The Temple in the House

FINDING
THE SACRED IN
EVERYDAY
ARCHITECTURE

The Temple in the House

ANTHONY LAWLOR, AIA

A Jeremy P. Tarcher/Putnam Book
published by
G. P. Putnam's Sons
New York

A Jeremy P. Tarcher/Putnam Book
Published by G. P. Putnam's Sons
Publishers Since 1838
200 Madison Avenue
New York, NY 10016

The author gratefully acknowledges permission to quote the following:

Eighteen lines from the Tao te Ching by Stephen Mitchell copyright © 1988 by Stephen Mitchell.
Reprinted by permission of HarperCollins Publishers, Inc.
"Stone" by Charles Simic © 1971, from *Dismantling the Silence,* reprinted by permission of George Braziller, Inc.
"Golden Lines" by Gerard de Nerval, translated by Robert Bly © 1980, from *News of the Universe.*
Reprinted by permission of Sierra Club Books.
"Unmarked Boxes" by Rumi, translated by John Moyne and Coleman Barks © 1984, from *Open Secret: Versions of Rumi.*
Reprinted by permission of Threshold Books.
Passage from *Lame Deer, Seeker of Visions* copyright © 1972 by John Fire/Lame Deer and Richard Erdoes.
Reprinted by permission of Simon & Schuster, Inc.
Poems 4 and 5 from *The Kabir Book* by Robert Bly © 1977. Reprinted by permission of Beacon Press.

Lawlor, Anthony.
    The temple in the house : finding the sacred in everyday architecture / by Anthony Lawlor.
        p.   cm.
    "A Jeremy P. Tarcher/Putnam book."
    Includes bibliographical references and index.
    ISBN 0-87477-777-1 (alk. paper)
    1. Architecture and religion.   2. Spiritualism (Philosophy)
I. Title.
NA4600.L38   1994   94-6985 CIP
720'.1'04—dc20

Design by Susan Shankin
Cover photographs by Anthony Lawlor
Photograph of the author by Rick Donhauser

Printed in the United States of America
1   2   3   4   5   6   7   8   9   10

This book is printed on acid-free paper.
∞

FOR THOSE WHO ENDEAVOR TO DWELL IN THE SACRED
and
SUZANNE, WHO INSPIRES THE JOURNEY
and
MY PARENTS, WHO SET ME ON THE WAY

Nothing is quite beautiful alone;
nothing but is beautiful in the whole.
A single object is only so far beautiful as
it suggests this universal grace.
The poet, the musician, the architect
seek to concentrate
this radiance of the world on one point.
Ralph Waldo Emerson

Contents

Introduction

The Japanese tea master Sen no Rikyu built a teahouse on the side of a hill overlooking the sea. Three guests were invited to the inaugural tea ceremony. Hearing about the beautiful site, they expected to find a structure that took advantage of the wonderful view. After arriving at the garden gate, they were perplexed to discover a grove of trees had been planted that obstructed the panorama. Before entering the teahouse, the guests followed the traditional custom of purifying their hands and mouths at the stone basin near the entry. Stooping to draw water with a bamboo ladle, they noticed an opening in the trees that provided a vision of the sparkling sea. In that humble position they awakened to the relationship between the cool liquid in the ladle and the ocean in the distance, between their individuality and the ocean of life.

Finding sacredness in common places is the subject of this book. Its goal is to reveal the temple of inspiration and renewal that is hidden within the walls of your house and city. You enter this temple by discovering a new way of seeing, one that reconnects the needs of your soul with the buildings and landscapes that shelter you. The following pages explore how architecture can become an ally in regaining wholeness in mind, body, and environment. They offer a guide to dwelling in the sacred places of the here and now, the everyday architecture of home and community.

The process of connecting consciousness and architecture supports the growing movement toward healing the fundamental disease of our time, the fragmentation of the world into isolated parts. The split between human beings and nature, mind and body, spirit and matter has generated damaging conflicts at every level of life. Human clashes with nature have fouled the earth's ecology to the point where

We see the world piece by piece,
as the sun, the moon,
the animal, the tree; but the
whole, of which these
are the shining parts, is the soul.
Emerson

The new era is the
era of spiritual creativity.
Henry Miller

our very survival is at stake. The division of mind and body has spawned neuroses and stress-related illnesses. The industrial culture that separates spirit from matter has left us wandering in an alienated, mechanistic wasteland. Style and economics are favored over content. What a building looks like and costs takes precedence over its effect on the total well-being of those who dwell or work within it. As a result we are surrounded by housing developments, office blocks, and towns that efficiently store people and automobiles but neglect the human need to nourish the soul.

In response to this fragmentation, many individuals and groups are working to mend the torn fabric of modern life, seeking sources of healing and renewal. Social action and ecological awareness are revitalizing society and the environment. Holistic medicine and psychology, meditation, and yoga are finding widespread use in the endeavor to integrate mind and body. Ancient mythologies are being studied with the hope of understanding how human life fits into the patterns and totality of existence.

These endeavors, however, do not usually include the architecture of homes and cities. A person might search for emotional healing or spiritual insight, perform community service, or simply recycle old newspapers, but it is business as usual when he or she furnishes a house or walks through the streets of a city. Yet architecture, instead of being a mere tool of form and function, can play a key role in renewing the spirit. Through the precise language of form, color, and texture, buildings ground the elusive qualities of consciousness in the physical world. Unlike philosophy, which is descriptive, architecture can provide a direct experience. A story about the soul's journey through the various stages of realization may provide knowledge; climbing a towering flight of steps to a temple or church puts the experience deep into your bones. Talking about compassionate action is inspiring; a shelter for the homeless provides a concrete love that words cannot describe.

Architecture is a primal element of human existence; it has deep connections to the sacred powers of life. Except in the most benign climates, we need a roof for shelter from the sun and rain, walls to insulate from wind and cold, and windows and doors to gain light and air. Most of us spend our entire lives interacting with architecture and designed landscapes. We are born in hospitals, we live in houses and apartments, study in schools, play in parks, work in offices, worship in churches, and are buried among the neat rows in cemeteries.

Physical places become key reference points on the psychological map of our individuality—home, school, and the workplace are used as touchstones to define who we are. Think of the countless floors that have supported you, the walls and roofs that have sheltered you, the doorways that have opened, the windows that have offered sunlight and air. Because of the essential role that buildings and cities play in shaping human experience, architecture can be embraced as a basic constituent of mind/body wholeness, a fundamental aspect of dwelling in sacredness.

The sacred cannot be precisely defined. Each of us perceives it through the lens of a unique personal history. For me, sacredness is an experience of the inner radiance of life, the unseen force that transforms and nourishes the physical world but is never limited by it. There is always something more to it, a mystery that is never totally grasped. The Tao te Ching says the way of the sacred "is like a well: used but never used up. It is like the eternal void: filled with infinite possibilities. It is hidden but always present." Sacredness is not isolated to particular places or times. The sixteenth-century Indian poet Kabir explains that it is "in the next seat. [Its] shoulder is against yours." In the Thomas Gospel, Jesus says the sacred kingdom of heaven "is spread across the face of the earth, but men do not see it." Sacredness is like the breath that constantly sustains our life without our being aware of it. The sacred is found in everyday architecture when we bring our attention to this life-giving force, opening ourselves to receive its inspiration, peace, and renewal within the cluttered house of the world. Discovering this completeness, we dwell within the wholeness of mind, body, and nature.

In my architectural practice and the design classes I teach, I find that many people want to extend the search for sacredness to their homes and workplaces. They ask how buildings can be perceived and designed to reflect the transformations in consciousness they are experiencing. These people are looking beyond "This Old House" in the hope of finding a temple in the house. They are beginning to link the energies that animate their thoughts and actions to those that craft chairs, construct houses, and build towns. They want to know how the stages of transformation through which the psyche journeys— the pain of separation, the search for meaning, the trials of the path, and the resolution of unity—are reflected in the environments that shelter and sustain them. There is a growing desire for dwellings that are like the tea master's ladle, dipping into the vital waters of eternity.

The house is more than a box within which to live; it is a soul activity to be retrieved from the numbness of the world of modern objects.
Robert Sardello

Each room contains a mythic universe.
Robert Sardello

Sacredness is found
in everyday architecture
by perceiving the
relationships between the many
levels of its
totality—mind, body,
environment,
home, community, and cosmos.

In response to this call for wholeness, the book addresses the complete person. In Part One: The Temple of Mind, Body, and Environment, I discuss the extended house of human experience—the buildings, cities, and landscapes that define our personal and collective world. These chapters are organized as a journey from the innermost realms of thinking and feeling through the body's processes and actions and out to the natural environment. They reveal how consciousness, physiology, and climate form a temple of sacredness that shapes physical matter into architecture. Chapter One focuses on the relationship between consciousness and building form. Chapter Two relates a primal thought pattern—that of desiring, searching, and finding fulfillment—to the architectural pattern of gate, path, and lotus seat. Chapter Three connects two extremes of human experience—turning outward to the aspiration of a higher goal and turning inward to gain healing inspiration—to the forms of steeple and sanctuary. Chapter Four describes how spirit interacts with matter to create the eight elemental building blocks of architecture: floors, walls, pillars, roofs, space, doors and windows, ornament, and rooms. Moving to the realm of the body, Chapter Five shows how human form, movement, and biological processes link consciousness to architecture. From here the book travels into the natural environment, with Chapter Six discussing the ways that buildings can attune mind, body, and community to the rhythms of nature.

Part Two: Dwelling in the Sacred suggests ways of expressing the temple of mind, body, and environment in your home, city, and world. Chapter Seven offers a means of creating a personal sacred place that nourishes your individuality and connection to spirit. This notion is expanded to include the infrastructure of community in the following chapter; it discusses how collective consciousness shapes the architecture of the city. Chapter Nine concludes the journey by exploring the pathways through which sacredness can be perceived at the core of every physical form.

The material is conveyed by discussing the ways that basic patterns of human consciousness, such as the aspiration for more in life, give rise to extraordinary sacred places, like Gothic cathedrals. Providing clear diagrams of the relationship between mind and building form, such structures embody what Joseph Campbell calls mythic archetypes, "the secret opening[s] through which the inexhaustible energies of the cosmos pour into human cultural manifestation."

These sites are then linked to everyday architecture, like the steeply pitched gable of a Victorian house or the soaring pinnacle of a high-rise office tower.

Since the link between spirit and matter is a fundamental human concern, this work draws on literature, mythology, philosophy, and historic architecture from around the world. We will examine such varied structures as a Hopi kiva, the Roman Pantheon, and a skylit living room in order to discover shared design concepts, and relate the elemental patterns of human awareness described by the Vedas, Tao te Ching, Bible, Koran, and Native American peoples to timeless patterns of building and inhabiting. In making these connections, my intention is not to reduce the rich texture of human dwellings to a few easily definable forms. Instead, I try to locate the unifying and renewing powers that create a vast diversity of architecture.

Sacredness becomes a living reality when we learn to see its elusive qualities within physical form and develop the skills to shape the immediate surroundings in a holistic manner. It is found in everyday architecture through intention, perception, and appreciation. With the intent to discover it, ability to perceive it, and desire to appreciate it, the sacred is drawn to the surface of matter as oil is elicited from an olive. To assist in recognizing the sacred, each chapter concludes with a section called "Seeing and Creating," which suggests concrete ways of applying the material to your home and workplace.

Buildings can become tangible connectors of individual consciousness and matter, integrating mind, body, community, and nature. Sacred architecture throughout history displays this notion. Spend some time at Chartres Cathedral or the rock garden at Ryoan-ji and you will find that the old master builders developed the knowledge of dwelling in wholeness long ago. This is not to romanticize the past as an era of perfect harmony, but history records numerous instances when human dwellings and the daily activities that occurred within them were attuned to the workings of the soul. The study of sacred modes of living found in time-tested building traditions holds keys to revitalizing ourselves and our environment. In the twentieth century, architects such as Frank Lloyd Wright, Bernard Maybeck, and Louis Kahn applied the ageless principles of holistic design to contemporary life. Moving through their work is a journey through the nuances of totality. Each architectural gesture is part of a seamless interplay of being and becoming.

Architecture is the reaching out for the truth.
Louis Kahn

If the sacred is to be discovered or reaffirmed in this culture, it is to be found under the bed.
Lynda Sexson

Architecture is that great living creative spirit which from generation to generation, from age to age, persists, creates, according to the nature of man, and his circumstances as they change.
Frank Lloyd Wright

Yet we have forgotten the art of crafting stone and wood in patterns that urge us to look beyond rigid enclosures of form to a perception of the transcendent mystery of existence. When we do happen across an ancient cathedral in the midst of a city or find a garden aligned with the rising and setting of the sun, most of us do not have the eyes to recognize the signals they are giving us. The forms and spaces they use to enhance human well-being have been traded for sterile shapes that stifle and distort it. The keys to shaping brick and mortar into objects that express the radiance of consciousness have been lost in a contemporary worldview that puts matter in one corner of life and the spirit that animates it in another.

The primal templates of architectural design presented in this book offer a means of reconnecting spirit and matter. They are not the tenets of any one philosophy, religion, or school of thought, but are fundamental structures of human life. Just as different musical styles draw on the same scale of seven notes, diverse types of architecture combine basic, universal "notes" of design. The soaring jazz of a Manhattan skyscraper, the resonant chant of a Gothic cathedral, the operatic sweep of a Baroque palace, and the country twang of a cabin in the woods all draw on shared archetypes of human dwelling. These universal patterns of design weave consciousness and matter into the walls, roofs, gardens, cities, and other objects that compose the physical environment. They are principles of relationship that yoke each part of life to the whole.

When they are understood, simple designs start to glow with a vitality that transcends the color and texture of matter. Common things—the stones of a garden path that gently guide our steps, a pillar that willingly supports the weight of a beam, or the templelike contours of a rural barn—become symbols of nature's vital processes. Each grouping of form is seen as a reflection of the cosmos.

The following pages offer a glimpse into the heart of the world by providing stepping-stones through the borderland of spirit and matter. They invite you to discover threads of wholeness that are personally significant, explore new places that can awaken memories of the soul's ancient roots, and experience familiar settings from a perspective that allows them to glow with new life. Traveling through subtler regions of seeing and creating, the everyday becomes sacred.

PART ONE

The Temple of Mind, Body, and Environment

Spirit and Mortar

There is a cloud floating in this sheet of paper. Without a cloud, there will be no rain; without rain, the trees cannot grow; and without trees, we cannot make paper. If we look even more deeply, we can see the sunshine, the logger who cut the tree, the wheat that became his bread, and the logger's father and mother. Without all these things, this sheet of paper cannot exist. In fact we cannot point to one thing that is not here—time, space, the earth, the rain, the minerals in the soil, the sunshine, the cloud, the river, the heat, the mind. Everything co-exists with this sheet of paper. . . . We cannot just be by ourselves alone; we have to inter-be with every other thing.

THICH NHAT HANH
The Heart of Understanding

Architecture and thought are intimate partners. Every building is born in the mind of its creator. Pyramids, Greek temples, Gothic cathedrals, Japanese shrines, skyscrapers, shopping malls, gas stations, and houses were all conceived in a stirring of consciousness. The notion arose to "make a sacred place," "create a beautiful setting," "build a soaring structure," "establish a home for a family." From these seeds sprouted the planning and construction that developed into architecture. In fact, every detail, down to the smallest nail, started as a glimmer in the eye of its designer. Someone determined the best length for the nail's shaft and the most appropriate diameter of its head. Almost every object in our daily experience came into being through this process. The chair you are sitting in, your clothes, this book, are all the result of a complex series of actions that grew from an original flash of insight. Finding the sacred in architecture begins with an understanding of how consciousness shapes building form.

A piece of architecture grows from the desire to shape the world around us in ways that support our needs and dreams. We project our desires, which have no material shape or mass, into the material environment. The force of our thoughts moves our bodies into the actions that frame up walls around a living room, place shingles on a roof, or set tile in a bathroom. A desire to be warm and dry in the winter has no tangible existence; I cannot touch it or see it. This invisible impulse of consciousness motivates me to shape wood, glass, metal, and other materials into the walls, roof, and windows of a house. In the process my mind interacts with matter, and both are altered. If I want a soft place to sit, a firm surface for slicing a loaf of bread, or a smooth, waterproof tub for bathing, I search for the materials that contain these qualities. Goose down and cotton contain the characteristics of softness for cushions; oak has the right hardness for a cutting board; porcelain holds water in curving shapes that fit the contours of my body. Look around and you will find these sorts of connections between consciousness and matter in every object.

Three things are needed for beauty: wholeness, harmony, and radiance.
Thomas Aquinas

Reveal the nature of the wood, plaster, brick, or stone in your designs.
Frank Lloyd Wright

Every building is born in the mind of its creator. The carved ornament on the public library in Fairfield, Iowa, reflects how the elusive qualities of human consciousness are poured into stone and brick. Spirit transforms matter into places of dwelling.

When our consciousness projects itself into the environment, it is seeking to establish a dwelling place in the world. Walls and a roof are not the goal of building a house; the aim is to create a seat for consciousness. We want to put "a roof over our heads," and we do this by defining the physical boundaries that nurture our minds and bodies. A floor is made for support, a wall for enclosure, a roof for shelter, a window to receive light. These boundaries provide a framework for our way of perceiving the environment and for fulfilling our bodily needs. The floor is level for easy walking; the walls are arranged to separate the rooms according to their functions; window placement refers to the height of our eyes and captures a view we find pleasing.

In creating the boundaries that define architecture, we mix the information of our consciousness with the materials in the environment. Blending the idea of a building block that can be easily lifted into position with clay, water, and fire produces a brick. When a tree is merged with the idea of shedding rain, a shingle is created. Information is the key ingredient for making architecture out of these mixtures; without its organizing power, the raw substances would not be transformed into useful building materials. In fact, building a house, school, or other structure is essentially a process of informing the physical environment about our needs and dreams. A pile of bricks becomes a wall by virtue of the messages it receives from the mason who builds it. With a mortar joint he tells each brick to sit three eighths of an inch above the one below it, three eighths of an inch from those to the right and left. Through the sign language of his hands and trowel he imparts the knowledge of making an arched opening for a window, a curve to turn a corner, or a decorative molding around a door. Maybe he caps the wall with a special detail he learned from the person who taught him the trade, one passed down from masons who built the Colosseum in Rome. When the wall is completed, information continues to be added: the sun washes over the brick day after day, year after year, fading the color; rain and wind smooth it grain by grain; maybe ivy grows up the wall, leaving viny traces; children climb along the top, making a chip here and there. Layer upon layer of information gives the wall a character all its own.

The bricks also speak to the mason. If he doesn't listen to what they have to say, the wall may come down on top of him. Weight, texture, hardness, and limits of flexibility are part of the information the mason needs to receive from the bricks in order to work with them.

Into the object a person puts life. When a certain thing is made, it is at that time that life is put into it, which goes on and on like breath in the body.
Hazrat Inayat Khan

He needs to know how the bricks will accept the mortar, their strength in resisting the wind, their ability to shed rain, etc. Louis Kahn suggested that we have "conversations" with materials to discover their most appropriate uses. They go something like this:

> You say to brick, "What do you want, brick?"
> Brick says to you, "I like an arch."
> If you say to brick, "Arches are expensive, and I can use a concrete lintel over an opening. What do you think of that, brick?"
> Brick says, "I like an arch."

With this example Kahn is telling us that material objects contain information about the ways they can best be used. The brick likes an arch because it is strong when pressed against other bricks. An arch can span a great distance simply by letting a group of bricks press one against the other, allowing a heavy lump of clay to fly through the air in a beautiful curving shape. By understanding the qualities that give the brick its individuality, we can bring out its true nature and use it in glorious ways.

Thousands of years before Kahn had his conversations with bricks, builders in India expressed a similar relationship between consciousness and matter. The Agni Purana suggests that these words be spoken to the first bricks that are placed in a building: "O daughter of the sage Angiras. Thou unbroken, unhurt, and full in size, O Brick grant thou the desired object. I now install thee." The Satapatha Brahmana conveys the notion that each brick is a microcosm of the earth: "He lays down the Invincible Brick. The invincible one being the earth, it is the earth that he lays down." The Vedas raise the common brick to the highest state of consciousness—that of a deity: "To thee, O Goddess, O Brick, let us sacrifice with an oblation." Every building material has a wonderful story to tell, if we only listen. Charles Simic reveals the subtle messages contained in a rock in his poem called "Stone":

> From the outside the stone is a riddle;
> No one knows how to answer it.
> Yet within, it must be cool and quiet
> Even though a cow steps on it full weight,

By knowing one lump of clay you know the essence of all things made of clay, their differences being only in name and form. By knowing one nugget of gold you know the essence of all things made of gold, their differences being only in name and form.
Chandogya Upanishad

Beauty is but the sensible image of the infinite. Like truth and justice it lives within us; like virtue and moral law it is a companion of the soul.
George Bancroft

Even though a child throws it in a river;
The stone sinks, slow, unperturbed
To the river bottom
Where the fishes knock on it
And listen.

I have seen sparks fly out
When two stones are rubbed,
So perhaps it is not dark inside after all;
Perhaps there is a moon shining
From somewhere, as though behind a hill—
Just enough light to make out
The strange writings, the star-charts
On the inner walls.

We work with the stuff
of the soul by means of the
things of life.
Thomas Moore

The Smithsonian Arts
and Industries Building in
Washington, D.C., displays
the ability of brick to span
distances with the graceful
curve of an arch. Notice the
range of ornament created by
varying the depth and color
of the brickwork.

The deeper we look into the physical structure of architecture, the more we find that it is primarily a field of information. According to quantum physics, every atom of a building consists of subatomic particles whizzing around a void of empty space; this void is proportionately as large as the distance between galaxies. Dwelling in the vast spaces between subatomic particles are the nonmaterial laws of physics that guide the material world. Like the invisible field of gravity between the earth and its moon, these voids are not realms of nothingness; they are fields of energy and information. Since every material object is a collection of atoms, architectural elements such as pillars, stairs, kitchen cabinets, and doorknobs are essentially fields of energy and information.

*The carved details of a doorway
in Washington, D.C., hold
the memory of its maker's caring
attention. Imagine the
innumerable threshold
crossings, both mundane and
exceptional, that have taken
place here—the layers
of experience that define
this home.*

Kahn intuitively understood this when he said, "Architecture does not exist, only the spirit of architecture exists." Because a building springs from a thought in someone's mind, it is an extension of the spirit that animates our lives. As Frank Lloyd Wright aptly put it, "As no stream can rise higher than its source, no building can rise higher than the consciousness of its architect." The poem "Golden Lines" by Gerard de Nerval describes it this way:

"Astonishing! Everything is intelligent."—Pythagoras

Look carefully in an animal at a spirit alive;
every flower is a soul opening out into nature;
a mystery touching love is asleep inside metal.
"Everything is intelligent!" And everything moves you.

In that blind wall look out for the eyes that pierce you:
the substance of creation cannot be separated from a word . . .
Do not force it to labor in some low phrase!

Often a Holy Thing is living hidden in a dark creature;
and like an eye which is born covered by its lids,
a pure spirit is growing stronger under the bark of stones!

I began to study the nature of materials, learning how to see them. I learned to see brick as brick, to see wood as wood, and to see concrete, glass, or metal. . . . As I could now see, there could be no organic architecture where the nature of materials was ignored or misunderstood.
Frank Lloyd Wright

The spirit of a building is revealed through the architectural forms that give it structure. An imposing government edifice gives us one message through its forms, while a cottage by the sea gives us another. The government building might use a portico of massive columns, a flight of monumental stone steps, and a doorway that towers over the people who enter it. Interestingly enough, the summer cottage employs elements similar to those of the government building, but they are given a different accent. The porch of the cottage has columns that are slender and closer to the height of a person; the steps are made of wood and double as a cozy bench for a couple of friends to talk; the doorway is light and intimate.

By receiving and reflecting the information we feed into them, building elements become repositories for our thoughts and feelings. They hold and nurture the psychological energy that animates our ways of living. The doorway of a house, for example, contains a world of information about the people who live inside. An intricately carved oak panel and a polished brass knob are signs that the occupants have poured a great deal of creativity and intelligence into their home. Over time, more and more consciousness is poured into the doorway through the life experiences that are associated with it. The parents' return from their honeymoon, a daughter's first kiss, a son's departure on his first solo walk to school, the grandparents' yearly arrival at Thanksgiving, and other events might become associated with the doorway.

In other words, the doorway is the residue, the culmination, of all the information that was put into it. Just as Thich Nhat Hanh's piece of paper is the outcome of the interaction between clouds, rain, trees, sunshine, the logger, and numerous other influences, the doorway is the result of all the information poured into it. Within it are thoughts, such as the invitation to enter and the hope that friends will come to share in the life of the house. Processes of transformation are also there; the metal for the hinges was removed from the earth, refined, and forged into a shape that allows the door to open and close; if there is a glass panel in the door, it was originally sand that was melted in a furnace and molded into a sheet of transparent material.

When objects and forms act as repositories of meaning, they gain symbolic content, and archetypal building forms are no exception. Besides serving their practical function of shelter, these forms act as outer symbols of our inner consciousness. A floor is both a physical means of support and a tangible symbol of emotional stability; a wall offers a symbol of separation and enclosure; a roof represents nurturing shelter. Each of the other architectural elements in turn becomes a focal point for the thoughts and feelings that animate our lives.

Usually we limit our perception of symbols to a narrow range of forms—the flag, the cross, the dollar sign—but every object can be infused with symbolic content. An old baseball glove can become a symbol of a child's freedom and innocence; a sweater knitted by a friend can represent loving companionship. In his book *Lame Deer, Seeker of Visions*, Lame Deer explains how the most commonplace objects can hold profound symbolic content:

> What do you see here, my friend? Just an ordinary old cooking pot, black with soot and full of dents.
>
> It is standing on the fire on top of that old wood stove, and the water bubbles and moves the lid as the white steam

In the background of the whole process of creation is Primal Matter pulsating with its own life, vibrating with inherent force, seeded with potentialities. Creative heat, starting a new vibration in the Primal Matter, gives rise to creative desire, the will-to-be which acts as the seed of mind, the imaginative principle, and from this follows the entire series of creations of visible, tangible forms.
Rig Veda

*Stone carvings at Hampi,
India, display a dialogue
between spirit and matter.
The sculptor's consciousness
passed through his hands and
into the native rock,
suffusing the raw substance
with symbolic content.*

rises to the ceiling. Inside the pot is boiling water, chunks of meat with bone and fat, plenty of potatoes.

It doesn't seem to have a message, that old pot, and I guess you don't give it a thought. Except the soup smells good and reminds you that you are hungry. . . .

But I'm an Indian. I think about ordinary, common things like this pot. The bubbling water comes from the rain cloud. It represents the sky. The fire comes from the sun which warms us all—men, animals, trees. The meat stands for the four-legged creatures, our animal brothers, who gave of themselves so that we should live. The steam is living breath. It was water; now it goes up to the sky, becomes a cloud again. These things are sacred. Looking at that pot full of good soup, I am thinking how, in this simple manner, Wakan Tanka takes care of me. We Sioux spend a lot of time thinking about everyday things, which in our mind are mixed up with the spiritual. We see in the world around us many symbols that teach us the meaning of life. . . . You could notice if you wanted to, but you are usually too busy. We Indians live in a world of symbols and images where the spiritual and the commonplace are one. . . . To us they are part of nature, part of ourselves—the earth, the sun, the wind and the rain, stones, trees, animals, even little insects like ants and grasshoppers. We try to understand them not with the head but with the heart, and we need no more than a hint to give us the meaning.

Finding the sacred in everyday architecture is a discovery of the fundamental links between spirit and matter. Physical forms are basically concentrated information—consciousness locked in specific patterns of awareness. Walls, doors, and other building forms are the means by which our thoughts are extended into the environment, the Word made architectural flesh.

*Everything in life
is speaking, is audible,
is communicating,
in spite of its apparent silence.*
Hazrat Inayat Khan

*Any object, intensely
regarded, may be a gate of
access to the incorruptible
eon of the gods.*
James Joyce

*The artist is a receptacle for
emotions, regardless of whether
they spring from heaven, from
earth, from a scrap of paper,
from a passing face,
or from a spider's web.*
Pablo Picasso

12

Seeing and Creating

1. Find a piece of building or decorating material that appeals to you, such as wood, glass, marble, or wool. Get acquainted with the material's unique qualities—color, texture, weight, smell, sound when struck, hardness, flexibility, even taste. Imagine or research the process by which this material came into being. How did it come out of the earth? What processes did it go through to become a building material? Think of the people and circumstances that brought this material to its present condition. Instead of seeing it as a purely physical object, perceive the material as a package of information. In the manner of Louis Kahn, have a conversation with this material. Ask the material how it likes to be used. What shapes and purposes express its true nature? What displays the material's unique qualities? Try this with another material to experience the different information it contains.

2. Place a fork, spoon, and knife on a table in front of you. Notice that each utensil is made of the same metal but has a unique shape. See the information that passed from the mind, through the hand, and into the metal. The knife is shaped by the information of cutting and spreading, the spoon by the intelligence of scooping, the fork by the intentions of piercing and lifting. Perceive the information in the metal that passed into the fork, how the metal has the ability to take on various shapes and remain strong and smooth. Use the fork, spoon, and knife to eat a meal, thinking of the implements as bundles of consciousness rather than as material objects.

3. Shape a raw material such as yarn, fabric, wood, or clay into a useful object. During the process, become aware of how information flows from your mind, through your hands, and into the material. Notice how you receive information from the material by interacting with it, discovering its color, texture, ability to be shaped, sound when struck, and appropriate uses.

4. Find an object in your house that is meaningful to you. What memories and experiences have passed into this object and are reflected back to you? See how your consciousness transforms a lump of matter into a symbol of life experience.

Gate · Path · Lotus Seat

In the pasture of the world, I endlessly push aside the tall grass in search of the bull. Along the riverbank under the trees, I discover footprints! Here no bull can hide! His great will and power are inexhaustible. Mounting the bull I return homeward. Astride the bull, I reach home. I am serene. The bull too can rest. The dawn has come. In blissful repose, within my thatched dwelling, I have abandoned the whip and rope. This heaven is so vast no message can stain it.

FROM ''TEN BULLS'' BY KAKUAN
Zen Flesh, Zen Bones

Consciousness molds architectural form through a fundamental pattern of thinking—desire, search, and find. Every thought is a step in the mind's journey through this pattern. I may wish for more knowledge, food, love, health, or peace; each desire motivates me to seek out the thing I want until I eventually find it. Architecture externalizes this expedition of consciousness in the archetypal forms of gate, path, and lotus seat. Almost every structure, from cathedrals to cottages, uses this triad as an organizing design principle. Because this configuration mirrors the source, journey, and goal of the human spirit's adventure, this elemental pattern shows up whenever we give architectural form to inner stirrings of thought and feeling.

Before discussing the specific connections between the mind and the architecture of gate, path, and lotus seat, it may be helpful to see how the theme of wanting, seeking, and finding is used to describe a classic tale of the sacred, the Buddha's enlightenment. Following the

Mind and matter are essentially the same. The field experienced subjectively is the mind, objectively it is the world of material objects.
Yoga Vasistha

The value of a personal relationship to things is that it creates intimacy and intimacy creates understanding and understanding creates love.
Anaïs Nin

trail of this profound transformation in consciousness can provide a reference point for understanding the intimate connections between the mind and everyday architecture.

Everyone in the palace was fast asleep when Prince Gautama decided to carry out his plan. Silently the prince made his way through the darkened halls to the stables, where he saddled his horse, Kantaka. The horse and rider crept through the heavy gates guarding the outer walls of the palace compound. Throughout the night the prince followed a road to the east. Only the Milky Way lit his path. At daybreak the horse and rider lightly crossed a majestic river that bordered the king's realm. Safe in this new territory, the prince removed the saddle and bridle from his horse and with a joyous cry set the steed free. Then, removing a pair of scissors from his saddlebag, the prince sheared his royal locks.

Assuming the garments of a monk, he moved as a beggar through the world. During these years of apparently aimless wandering, he visited the learned teachers of the day, mastering the subtlest philosophies the mind could invent. After some time he retired to a hermitage and entered six years of purification and meditation. Then he returned to the less rigorous life of a wandering ascetic, following the promptings of his intuition.

One day the prince-turned-monk sat beneath a tree, appreciating the beauty of the sunrise. His generous smile seemed to be illuminating every leaf and branch. A young girl named Sujata came and offered the monk milk rice in a bowl tinged with the golden rays of the morning sun. When the meal was finished, he tossed the empty bowl into a river that ran by the tree. To his amazement, the bowl floated upstream. "Hmm," he thought, "this is the moment I have been waiting for." The monk stood up and walked along a road. The snakes, birds, insects, and other creatures of the woods and fields seemed to buzz with excitement. Flowers and grasses were radiant with color. A breeze rustled the trees into a heavenly chorus. The world was filled with perfumes, garlands, harmony, and shouts of acclaim. For he was about to reach the long-sought goal of his journey.

The monk rounded a bend in the trail and there it was—a magnificent bo tree, whose massive roots seemed to plunge deep into the earth and whose enormous, spreading branches appeared to touch heaven. Placing himself beneath this mighty tree, he made a firm resolve not to move from the spot until he attained full awakening. But no sooner had the sage settled beneath the bo tree than a horrific-looking demon approached. It was Kama-Mara, the god of love and death. The dangerous god rode a colossal elephant and was carrying treacherous weapons. He was surrounded by his army, which extended twelve leagues before him, twelve to the right, twelve to the left, and to the rear as far as the confines of the forest. The monk, however, remained calmly beneath the tree.

Then the god assailed him, seeking to shatter his concentration. The antagonist hurled at the sage a whirlwind of rocks, thunder, and flame, smoking weapons with keen edges, burning coals, boiling mud, blistering sands, and fourfold darkness. But the monk had learned many secrets during his wanderings. Raising his hand in a gesture of greeting, the missiles were transformed into celestial flowers and ointments. Kama-Mara then brought forth the powers of Desire, Pining, and Lust, surrounded by voluptuous attendants. But the monk remained calm and was not distracted. The demon finally challenged the monk's right to be sitting on the sacred spot. Flinging his razor-sharp discus with a scream, Kama-Mara bid his thousands of soldiers to descend upon the monk. But the sage merely touched the ground with his fingertips and thus bid the goddess Earth to bear witness to his right to be sitting where he was. She did so with a hundred thousand roars, so that the elephant of the antagonist fell upon its knees in obeisance to the monk and the army scattered in all directions.

Having cleared away the obstacles to his purpose, the sage let his mind settle into the depths of his consciousness. In the first watch of the night, all limitations of rigid thinking dissolved. In the second

There is something bigger and more worthwhile than the things we see about us, the things we live and strive for. There is an undiscovered beauty, a divine excellence, just beyond us. Let us stand on tiptoe, forgetting the nearer things, and grasp what we may.
Bernard Maybeck

17

watch, the divine eye of omniscient vision opened. And in the last, he perceived the interdependence of every being in the universe. At the break of day, he attained the perfect enlightenment of Buddhahood.

The story of Gautama Buddha's enlightenment is a mythic version of a journey we all take. We leave the familiar realm of our parents' house and enter new lands of hope and fear, companionship and isolation, love and hate, turmoil and peace—looking to establish our own place in the world. This journey begins by approaching a gate.

Inventories from children's hiding places and from religious holy places bear remarkable similarity.
Lynda Sexson

When a garden is used as a place to pause for thought, that is when a Zen garden comes to life. When you contemplate a garden like this it will form a lasting impression in your heart.
Muso Soseki

GATE

He brought me to the gate . . . that looketh toward the east:
And, behold, the glory of the God of Israel came from the
way of the east: and his voice was like a noise of many waters:
and the earth shined with his glory.　**Ezekiel**

Desire is the primal impulse of the mind. Before any action takes
place, the urge to transform familiar conditions rises within us. This
primal impulse in consciousness takes architectural form as the gate.
Over the gate of Obaku Temple in Kyoto there are large carved
characters that spell out "The First Principle." The gate illustrates experiences of transcendence, the departure from one configuration of
objects and circumstances to another. Offering a promise, a lure, the
gate invites us to let the spiritual trek begin. It is a transfer of em-
phasis from the external to the internal, at once a symbol of death and
resurrection, an opening through which the inexhaustible energies of
the cosmos pour into human life. The Zen master Hakuin once offered a beautiful insight into the subtle energies that design gates.

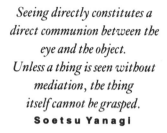

*Seeing directly constitutes a
direct communion between the
eye and the object.
Unless a thing is seen without
mediation, the thing
itself cannot be grasped.*
Soetsu Yanagi

*The ornate details and height
of this Japanese gate indicate
its architectural importance.
Those bowing before it
acknowledge its significance
as an emblem of inner
transformation.*

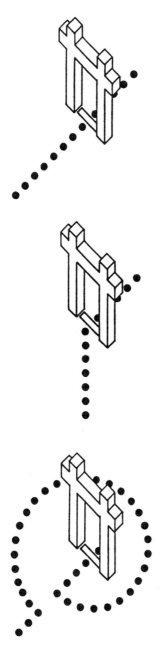

Three types of approach:
frontal, oblique, and spiral.

A soldier named Nobushige asked Hakuin, "What is the difference between heaven and hell?"

"Don't bother me with such stupid questions," said Hakuin. "Beggars like you have no use for such knowledge."

"But I am a samurai," the warrior replied. "And it is essential that I know the answer to this question."

"You a soldier!" cried Hakuin. "Who could you defeat in a battle? No ruler would be safe with you in his army."

Nobushige was enraged and reached for his sword. But Hakuin continued, "What's that, a sword? Did you steal that from a real samurai?"

Nobushige began to draw his sword and Hakuin calmly remarked, "This opens the gates of hell."

Stunned by the master's steadiness and wisdom, the samurai sheathed his sword and bowed.

"This opens the gates of heaven," said the master.

A gate frames its invitation by using precise components—an approach, twin pillars, crossbeam, door, latch, key, hinge, and threshold. The approach rolls out the red carpet in the call to expansion of life experience. It is the steps of the temple, the garden path in the front yard, the trail that disappears into the deep woods. There are essentially three ways of approaching a gate: the direct frontal assault of a straightaway path; the oblique sidestep that delays the approach and reveals new perspectives of experience; or the curving spiral that meanders about before entering. Pennsylvania Avenue in Washington, D.C., is a direct approach to Capitol Hill. A diagonal path reaches obliquely toward the Parthenon in Athens. The customary path into an Indian temple is a clockwise circuit around its mass before entering the portal.

Bordering the gate, the twin pillars guard the opening to new awareness, embodying life and death, beauty and ugliness, good and evil, hope and fear, and the other polarities that bind us to a limited existence. You may want to go, but you want to stay. You love him, but you hate him. To be or not to be . . . The Greeks associated duality with two rock islands between which the hero Jason sailed. The entrances to Buddhist temples are often flanked by two statues representing fear and desire, warding off those too fainthearted to make the spiritual quest.

The rocky ascent to a gate on Mount Sinai reflects the inner experience of the pilgrims who approach it.

This mountain of release is such that the ascent is most painful at the start, below; the more you rise, the milder it will be. And when the slope feels gentle to the point that climbing up sheer rock is effortless as though you were gliding downstream in a boat, then you have arrived at where the path ends.
Dante

21

Two statues representing fear and desire guard a Japanese gate (right). Male and female become the twin pillars in a Brookline, Massachusetts, garden (lower right). Whalelike pillars define a gate from the remains of a Kwakiutl house in the Pacific Northwest (opposite).

*The things of this world
are vessels, entrances for
stories; when we touch them,
we fall into their labyrinthine
resonances. The world is no
longer divided, then, into those
inconvenient categories of
subject and object, and the
world becomes religiously
apprehended.*
Lynda Sexson

The crossbeam spans the gulf between the gate's twin pillars, uniting the space between them. It marks the upper limit of the gate and focuses attention on the transforming tasks of the path ahead. The cross created by the meeting of beam and pillar is said to symbolize the passage into the transcendent, the mysterious boundary between inner and outer worlds.

In Asia, the Face of Glory adorns the crossbeams of many temples. Symbolic of the "match for any evil," it recalls the story of a king who had the impudent idea of asking the god Shiva to give him his wife, Parvati. The king sent Rahu—"the Seizer," who eclipses the sun and moon—as a messenger to make his demand of Shiva. When the god heard this bold request, he widened the third eye between his eyebrows and shot forth a bolt of lightning that struck the earth and then took the form of a lion-headed demon. The monster's gaunt, emaciated body radiated an insatiable hunger. Its throat gave a thunderous roar, its eyes blazed with fire, its wild mane seemed to fill the sky. The demon's strength was so terrifying that Rahu begged Shiva for mercy and was granted protection. But the ravenous half lion was left with nothing to eat. When he turned to Shiva for help, the god suggested that the demon eat his own body. Beginning with his feet, he began the bizarre feast. The monster munched his way up his own legs and through his stomach, chest, and neck until there was nothing left but a face. Shiva, who had been watching this display of life's self-consuming mystery, smiled and said, "You shall be known as Kirttimukha, 'Face of Glory,' and shall always live over my door. No one who fails to worship you will ever obtain my grace."

Then said the Lord unto me: This gate shall be shut, it shall not be opened, and no man shall enter in by it. . . . It is for the prince . . . he shall enter by the way of the porch of that gate, and shall go out by the way of the same.   **Ezekiel**

*The Eye of Horus adorning the
crossbeam of the Egyptian
Temple of Isis unified the twin
pillars supporting it.*

A crossbeam at 30 Rockefeller
Plaza in New York displays
a mythic figure using a compass
to establish points of stability
amid the waves of
transformation that sweep
across modern life, while
a proverb reminds passersby
of the powers of wisdom
and knowledge.

Beauty—the
adjustment of all parts
proportionately so
that one cannot add or
subtract or change
without impairing the
harmony of the whole.
Alberti

Worshippers entering Chartres Cathedral pass beneath a figure of Christ, surrounded by a bull, a lion, an eagle, an angel, and a host of saints (right). The self-consuming mystery of life is portrayed by the bulging eyes and gaping mouth of the Face of Glory on a crossbeam at Borobudur in Java (opposite).

Hindering the passage through the gate are the door and latch. They represent the veil and challenge posed by rigid patterns of thinking. The door blocks and opens, intimidates and welcomes. Its lock is the first barrier to overcome, the mystery to be solved. Edged in hardened steel, it can only be opened by piercing the darkness at its center. At a temple in Japan, visitors are invited to find a hidden lock within a lightless tunnel under the building's main structure. A man, terrified of the dark, struggled through the ordeal but only encountered his fear. He happened to mention to one of the monks at the temple that he had failed to find the fabled lock. The monk replied, "The entirety of that dark passage is the lock." The mind and body of this spiritual tourist turned out to be the key.

Opening the way to the path of self-discovery, the key symbolizes new insights and techniques for awakening consciousness. Inserting a key into a lock symbolizes the entry of mind and body through a gate. Meditation, yoga, and other techniques are instruments for unlocking the mind's abilities.

Hinges allow the gate to open. Their stable pins and swinging leaves are similar to the ability of consciousness to flow in patterns of active thought while remaining centered in calm stability. As the Indian story goes, Brahma sits on a lotus in heaven: every time his eyes open, a universe is born; every time they close, a universe dissolves. Creation comes and goes through the gate on the hinge of an eyelid. Breathing in and breathing out swings the doorway of living.

When the catalyst for transformation has done its work, the threshold of the gate is crossed. Marking the transfer of a spiritual center of gravity from the known to the unknown, the threshold of-

Doors possess magical qualities in stories and fairy tales and folklore. They are entrances through which imagination moves.
Robert Sardello

The latch on the door to Rouen Cathedral recalls the entire building in miniature. Its ornamentation is similar to the tracery of the cathedral's immense stained-glass windows.

fers the initial step into the sacred zones of consciousness. The subtle design of the threshold leading to a Japanese tea garden is a little poem of hospitality. Outside the bamboo gate is a large stone called the guest stone. A threshold stone indicates the line between the chaos of the external world and the tranquillity of the garden within. Inside the gate, the host stone is dropped several inches below the guest stone it faces, making a deferential gesture of welcome. The threshold is perpendicular to the path that crosses it, creating a sort of compass that points to the four corners of the world.

Opposites seem to be products of partial cognition and fade away with cognition of the whole.
Abraham Maslow

The solid oak planks and wrought-iron hinges indicate a firm yet movable barrier to the doorway of a gardener's shed at Dumbarton Oaks in Washington, D.C.

29

Nothing is quite beautiful alone; nothing is beautiful but in the whole. A single object is only so far beautiful as it suggests this universal grace. The poet, the musician, the architect seek each to concentrate this radiance of the world on one point.
Emerson

PATH

A Navajo legend describes the time when the Twin War Gods traveled to the house of their father, the Sun, by following a sacred path. The boys moved along the path and after sunrise saw smoke rising from the hole of an underground chamber. Inside the chamber was the Spider Woman, who looked at them and said, "Welcome, children, come in. Where are you going?" The boys remained silent as they descended the ladder that poked through the smoke hole. When they reached the floor she again asked them their destination.

The boys would not reveal their goal, but the old woman said, "I get the feeling you are looking for your father?"

"Yes," they answered, "but we don't know where to find him."

"The way to your father's house is long and perilous," said the old woman. "Demons guard the way and your father may be angry at you. The path has four places of danger—crushing rocks, cutting reeds, tearing cane cactuses, and boiling sands. But I will give you weapons to defeat your enemies and sustain your lives." She gave them a hoop and two feathers plucked from the tail of a living eagle, and another feather to replenish their strength. She also taught them a secret incantation to subdue the rage of their enemies: "Put your feet down with pollen. Put your hands down with pollen. Put your head down with pollen. Then your feet are pollen; your hands are pollen; your body is pollen; your mind is pollen; your voice is pollen. The trail is beautiful. Be still."

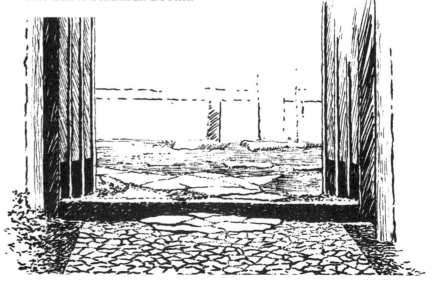

At the Katsura Imperial Villa, the guest stone in the foreground announces the moment of arrival at the keen-edged, geometric line of the threshold. The host stone and meandering stones beyond it indicate entry into a new realm of experience.

A colonnade at Dumbarton Oaks, in Washington, D.C., embodies the rhythms of transformation along the path.

Even the common articles made for daily use become endowed with beauty when they are loved.
Soetsu Yanagi

Three types of path configuration: linear, radial, and spiral.

Representing the initiation, journey, and time of transformation, the path symbolizes psychological, not physical, triumphs. It provides a way to gain knowledge and awaken consciousness. Along the way obscure resistances are overcome and long-lost powers are revived. The snags and stumbling blocks of doubt, disappointment, and resistance may obstruct the path, but the ancient wisdom whispers that we only have to know and trust, for helpers will appear.

The Twin War Gods in the Navajo story were assisted in their quest to reach the house of the Sun not only by the wisdom and magic formula of the Spider Woman but also by specially designed objects in the physical environment. The wise crone resided in a subterranean chamber—the womb of matter, the sanctuary hidden beneath the comings and goings of the mundane world. A ladder signaled the way and provided a means to reach the transcendental realm. In order to overcome the trials of the journey, she gave the boys the material design of wholeness—a hoop—and physical objects that were imbued with vitality—two feathers plucked from a living eagle. The magic formula for subduing the anger of their enemies describes direct connections between energy and matter. Pollen symbolizes life, the energy that impregnates the pistil of the flower to produce the seeds of a new generation. Spider Woman urges them to "put their feet down with pollen," to connect their physical bodies to the materiality of the path and the vital energies of life. As we will see in a later chapter, architecture can embody this formula by serving as a link between mind, body, and the natural environment.

Architecture can shape the route to transformation out of the tangible stuff of our everyday lives. A winding trail in the park, a street rolling through the canyons of a city, or a stair ascending to a second-floor bedroom are outward reflections of the path to enlightenment. Outer and inner paths are constructed of five elements that mold the experiences of the journey: configuration, stepping-stones, bridges, stairs, and layers of unfolding.

The shifts from disappointment to hope, from desperation to fulfillment, and from ignorance to knowledge are experiences that indicate the configuration of consciousness as it flows along the path. During this journey, our thought patterns tend to take three shapes: linear, radial, and spiral. A linear path leads step-by-step to the resolution of a conflict. This is mirrored by the corridors of buildings and country roads edged by forests. Consciousness can move radially by traveling inward to a centered spot or outward to enrich the world. The journey of Gautama Buddha gathered the energies of his early life on the Immovable Spot, the point from which he radiated them to all sentient beings. In Paris, a number of boulevards emanate from the Arc de Triomphe; all roads once led to Rome. Spiral paths map a stream of consciousness that expands to new dimensions while referring to the source of its existence. Any point on a spiral displays the history of past actions that led to that spot and indicates the direction of future growth.

When various paths intersect, a network configuration is formed. Distinct energies are combined and lines of communication are opened, giving rise to vital points of experience. Crossing the paths of a man and woman may result in the birth of a child, generating the web of family life. In rural areas, the marketplace of goods, services, and knowledge is usually stationed at a crossroads. The overlapping of two or more paths alters the character of each. When the trails of teacher and student meet, both lives are changed; pathways of thought and feeling are transformed through giving and receiving. Buildings located at the convergence of city streets often have unusually shaped corners that acknowledge the intertwining energies of the boulevards. Acting as the acupuncture points of the network, these synergistic spots influence the experiences on the paths leading up to them. A rush-hour traffic jam at a downtown intersection, for example, can clog a city's arteries, spreading frustration in every direction. In a network configuration, consciousness can be transformed from small-minded, selfish concerns to the all-embracing compassion of the whole. The struggle of "looking out for number one" becomes the mutual support of "one for all, all for one." The invisible web of intelligence that connects disparate paths allows each individual to transcend isolation and incompleteness.

The connections of a network are vital to the existence of each individual, for without them, the energies that sustain life cannot flow in nourishing channels. One of the oldest strategies of war involves blocking the path of supplies in order to starve out the enemy. Internal wars that congest the body can cause heart attacks, pneumonia, or kidney problems. A convoluted or murky network of paths creates labyrinthine structures—places where primal forces are constrained in mysterious twists and turns. The story of King Minos provides a classic illustration of these distorted energies.

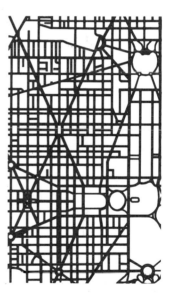

In Washington, D.C., intersecting paths form a network. The U.S. Capitol, White House, and other centers of interaction are linked by diagonal boulevards that cut through the orthogonal grid of streets.

Minos competed with his brothers for the throne of Crete and maintained that it was his by divine right. He prayed to Poseidon for a sign of affirmation, a bull rising out of the sea. The would-be king vowed to sacrifice the animal to show his loyalty to Poseidon. The god produced the bull, making Minos the ruler. But the beast's magnificent stature filled the new king with the desire to keep it. So Minos decided to risk substituting the finest white bull of the royal herd, hoping that Poseidon would not mind the replacement.

Under the wise rule of Minos, the Cretan empire flourished. The nation's influence extended to the edges of the known world. But Poseidon wanted to even the score for the broken verbal contract. The god planted in the heart of Minos' wife, Pasiphaë, an uncontrollable desire for the bull. She summoned the royal architect, Daedalus, to fashion a wooden cow that would attract the animal. She entered the decoy and the bull was deceived. In time Pasiphaë gave birth to a son who had a human body but the head and tail of a bull—the Minotaur, which became dangerous as it grew. The horrified King Minos summoned Daedalus and asked him to build a vast labyrinth where the thing could be hidden away. The structure fulfilled its purpose so well that Daedalus himself barely found his way out when it was finished. The Minotaur settled into the bowels of the labyrinth's tangled web of paths. There he was fed with groups of living youths who were brought from other conquered nations.

A labyrinth embedded in the floor of Rheims Cathedral signifies the relationship of Gothic architects to the legendary Daedalus. The names of the four architects who designed the cathedral are inscribed in the four corners (below). A Pima basket recalls the path of an individual soul through the labyrinth of the world (right).

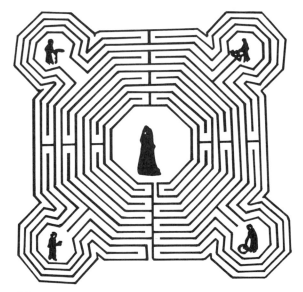

The architects who supervised the construction of Rheims Cathedral in the thirteenth and fourteenth centuries acknowledged their connection to the legendary Daedalus by embedding the design of a labyrinth in the floor. In English gardens, mazes formed by boxwood hedges invite country visitors to experience a tangle of paths. In the Middle Ages, such labyrinths were used for penance; the penitent had to make his way through them until he finally discovered the symbolic representations of Jerusalem, heaven, or a saint at the center. These labyrinths are descendants of those used in Egypt and Mesopotamia to safeguard the king's tombs, symbolically placed at the center of the greatest of mysteries, life and death. The builders of these convoluted structures entered the knotted passages in order to renew and strengthen their own vitality by associating with the immortal lives of their ancestors.

Daedalus not only built the labyrinth for King Minos, he also provided a way to pass through it to freedom. Ariadne, the daughter of the king, fell in love with Theseus, one of the youths brought to meet his fate with the Minotaur. She told him she would help him out of the labyrinth if he would promise to take her away from Crete and marry her. Theseus agreed, and Ariadne sought the help of Daedalus. The architect gave her a skein of linen thread, which Theseus could fasten to the entrance and unwind as he went into the maze, then follow in reverse when he wanted to return to the light.

It's not the road you walk, it is the walking.
Vatsyayana

If you dug up a tarnished mirror of periods thousands of years ago, you could re-enact the use of the mirror.
Louis Kahn

In Los Angeles, hundreds of thousands of vehicles pass through this labyrinthine freeway interchange each day.

35

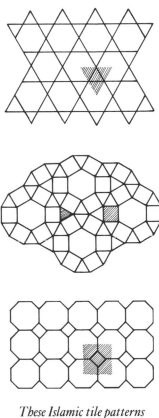

These Islamic tile patterns display the power of the triangle and square to generate networks that are orderly yet dynamic. Each point of intersection in the network reflects every other intersection, creating a system of mutual support.

When the nodal points of a network allow energy to pass through them without restriction, the twists and turns of the labyrinth are clarified and the entire system sparkles with vitality. This idea is portrayed in India as the mythic image of the Net of Indra, a net of gems. At every crossing of one thread over another, there is a gem mirroring all the other reflective gems. A condition arises in which everything is seen in relation to everything else—a system of mutual support. A field of innumerable points is mirrored at every single point. The universe is reflected in each grain of sand, drop of dew, and beat of the heart.

The path can employ four elements to give it physical form—stepping-stones, bridges, stairs, and layers of unfolding. Stepping-stones provide tangible support for the journey. They are helpers that uphold the traveler's progress and guide his or her way by offering clues to future development. In the Navajo legend, Spider Woman's wisdom made stepping-stones of knowledge for the Twin War Gods. Daedalus' thread gave Theseus the clue he needed to negotiate the labyrinth with safety. Stepping-stones can be placed side by side to create the smooth pavement of concrete walks, brick paths, and tile flooring—an arrangement that facilitates rapid progress. They can also be separated in the measured tread of walking. Japanese gardens use both of these arrangements. On the solid pavement it isn't necessary to watch your step. Your awareness can expand to encompass the various arrangements of trees, shrubs, and flowers. When traversing a group of stepping-stones scattered on a carpet of moss, however, care must be taken to avoid slipping; awareness is focused on each step. Alternating solid pavement with separated stones causes consciousness to fluctuate between expansion and contraction.

Sometimes the path is blocked by a precipice, a raging river, or some other obstacle. Chasms of rigid thinking or rushes of fear can seem like insurmountable barriers until a bridge of knowledge is found. At the beginning of his journey, Gautama Buddha crossed to the shore of enlightenment on the back of his horse. A ladder allowed the Twin War Gods to span from the visible world of mundane form to the hidden domain of the interior world. Persian mythology describes the Cinvat Bridge that is crossed by the dead; for the just this bridge is said to be nine lance lengths wide, but for the wicked it becomes as narrow as "the blade of a razor." Beneath it is the mouth of hell. The vision of Saint Paul speaks of a bridge "as narrow as a hair"

These stepping-stones
at Katsura Imperial Villa
scattered in an angular
arrangement force the traveler
to focus attention on each
step of the path.

At the Katsura Imperial Villa, the stones of the solid pavement are carefully joined, allowing one's attention to take in the surrounding garden.

that connects earth with heaven. Stories of the Middle Ages tell us about a "bridge under water" and of the sword bridge that Lancelot crossed with his bare feet and hands. The Katha Upanishad says the bridge to spiritual transformation is "a sharpened edge of a razor." Through the wisdom of self-discovery, we can bridge the obstacles to our awakening. Sometimes it just takes a leap of faith.

The Drum Bridge gracefully spans a waterway in Osaka, Japan.

When the path leaves the plane of horizontal movement to rise or fall in ascending or descending stages of progression, it takes the form of stairs. Climbing a flight of rickety steps to an attic can be a withdrawal from routine activities to a region of expansive dreams. Here the air is a mist of dust; the earth and its concerns seem far below. The stone stairs to a cellar descend to the murky realms within the ground. The air is dank; water and earth merge in dense stability.

In architecture and consciousness, the path is traversed by moving through layers of unfolding. Think of all the rooms you pass through in a single day—from the bedroom through the bathroom, to the living room and kitchen, the city streets, the office, a restaurant, and so on. Each room has its own distinct flavor, mirroring the layers of experience that open to new insights and knowledge. From the privacy and silence of home to the crowds and noise of the street and city, the mind can travel through veils of anticipation, hope, exhilaration, doubt, disappointment, anger, pain, and the healing resolution of peace. In meditation, thinking moves from active turbulence on the surface of the mind to silent unity in its depths.

Japanese gardens ask that you go beyond the garden spiritually. That you look at the garden not merely as an object but also as a path into the realms of the spirit.
Makoto Ooka

A staircase spirals from the ground level to the third story of this Shaker building.

The emergence design depicts the Pueblo Indian myth of human beings rising from the underworld.

Vézelay Cathedral in France vividly portrays the way architecture can reflect the journey of the spirit through ignorance to enlightenment. We enter through a darkened, cavelike porch. Moving along the row of pillars framing the central aisle, we are bathed in a medium intensity of illumination. When we arrive at the altar, our senses are flooded with the dazzling rays of the sun. Along the way our awareness is broadened. Our mind shifts from the solidity of matter to the luminosity of transcendental things.

Emanuel Swedenborg wrote about passing through layers of consciousness in a dream on the night of October 19–20, 1744: "I saw one beast after another, and they spread their wings and were dragons. I was flying over them, but one of them was supporting me." The Koran offers the reminder that mythic figures and saints are not the only ones who must journey through layers of experience to reach fulfillment: "Do you think that ye shall enter the Garden of Bliss without such trials as came to those who passed before you?" The following legend of the Bride of Mero beautifully renders the sequential unfolding of deeper layers of thinking and feeling.

In parts of ancient China, there was a time when the path of self-awakening was forgotten and people devoted themselves only to materialistic pursuits. But the goddess Kuan-yin led the people to illumination in the following way.

Early one day, a young woman of the finest beauty and grace carried a basket of woven bamboo into a village in the western provinces. It was lined with green leaves and filled with fresh golden-scaled fish. As she announced her wares her voice suggested the play of a delicate wind chime. The villagers gawked and gossiped among themselves, but none of them recognized her.

Every morning she appeared. As soon as her basket was emptied, the young woman would disappear so quickly that the people sometimes doubted she had been there at all. A group of young men took notice of her and waited for her daily appearances. One morning they blocked her path and began begging her to marry them. Calmly she replied, "I would like to marry you, but I cannot become the wife of so many young men. If one of you, however, could recite the entire Sutra of the Compassionate Kuan-yin by heart, I would marry him."

The minds of those young men were so clouded by ignorance that they had never even heard of that sutra. Nevertheless, they met that evening to recite the sutra. By the next morning, thirty had memorized the text. As they surrounded the young woman she said, "But I am only one woman; I cannot marry thirty of you. However, I will marry the young man who can explain the meaning of the sutra."

The following dawn ten men waited to explain the meaning and marry the young woman. But she replied, "There is only one of me. How can I marry ten husbands? However, I will marry the man who experiences the meaning of the Sutra of the Compassionate Kuan-yin in three days."

On the morning of that third day, just one remained, the young Mero. When the young woman saw him there, she smiled. "O Son of the House of Me," she said, for she could discern the features of his lineage, "I see that you have realized the meaning of the Sutra of the Compassionate Kuan-yin. Come to my house at the river bend this evening to meet my parents and I will take you as my husband."

At dusk, Mero went to the bend in the shore. There he discovered the young woman's little house among the reeds and rocks. By the gate stood an old man and woman, calling to him. He approached and said to them, "I am the son of the House of Me and have come to claim your daughter as my bride."

You and I are molded by the land, the trees, the sky and all that surrounds us, the streets, the houses. . . . Our hearts are shaped by the plaster walls that cover us and we reflect plaster wall ideals. . . . When I make a vase, a cup, or a saucer, they will be my expression and they will tell you who I am and what I am.

Bernard Maybeck

41

The old man responded, "We have been waiting for you for a long time. Please come in."

The old woman led the way into the house and opened the door to her daughter's room. Mero went in, but the room was empty. Through an open window he saw a stretch of sand leading to the river, and in the sand the footprints of a woman. He followed them to the water's edge and found two golden sandals. He turned around to find that the house among the rocks had disappeared. Only a cluster of dry bamboo by the river rustled softly in the evening breeze. And then the realization dawned. The fisher maid had been none other than Kuan-yin in human form. Now he fully comprehended the infinite compassion of the goddess who had fashioned a bridge of love that led him to the shore of awakening.

Architecture is the handwriting of man. . . . When you enter his domain you know . . . his dreams.
Bernard Maybeck

Pilgrims pass through the layers of gate, stairway, and circular terrace to reach the Buddhist stupa at Sanchi, India.

Ignorance, struggle, the figuring of the mind, and the moods of the heart are footprints that traverse the unfolding layers of consciousness, bringing us to the peaceful shore. According to Joseph Campbell in *The Hero with a Thousand Faces,* "We have not even to risk the adventure alone; for the heroes of all time have gone before us; the labyrinth is thoroughly known; we have only to follow the thread of the hero-path. And where we thought to find an abomination, we shall find a god; where we thought to slay another, we shall slay ourselves; where we thought to travel outward, we shall come to the center of our own existence; where we thought to be alone, we shall be with all the world." Here the trail arrives at a place of revolution. The next step leaves the trials and boundaries of the path and brings us to the expansive home of the sacred.

In one way or another, the Cosmos we inhabit—human body, house, territory, world—communicates from above with another level which is transcendent.
Mircea Eliade

The path of spiritual transformation travels through layer after layer of unfolding. The statues and painted arches of the grand staircase of the Seattle Art Museum by Venturi, Scott Brown and Associates give this theme a tangible form.

LOTUS SEAT

The path points the way to the goal. Techniques for transforming mind and body, as well as intellectual knowledge, are merely vehicles for ferrying us to the luminous shore of truth, consciousness, and bliss. Eventually it is time to occupy the lotus seat of fulfillment. Prince Gautama claimed his right to the Immovable Spot under the bo tree and was transformed into a living Buddha. Moses' climb up Mount Sinai culminated in his beholding the face of God. The son of the House of Me followed the trail of love until he found a pair of golden sandals pointing to the all-embracing benevolence of infinite compassion.

The lotus seat signals arrival at the goal. Here the contradictions of the path are transcended, unity is discovered, and peaceful fulfillment is achieved. Something that blazed invisibly within the material world breaks forth, and the conflicting shadows of the journey are dispelled by the illumination of the soul. It is a return to the source, rebirth, the recovery of self—an experience the Mundaka Upanishad describes in this way:

> He who finds it is free; hc has found himself; he has solved the great riddle; his heart is forever free. Whole, he enters the Whole. His personal self returns to its radiant, intimate, deathless source . . . he passes beyond all suffering, beyond death; all the knots of his heart are loosed.

In a clean place, having set his seat firm, neither very high nor very low, having placed sacred grass, deerskin, and cloth one upon the other. Seated there on the seat, having made the mind one-pointed, with the activity of the senses and thought subdued, let him practice Yoga for self-purification.
Bhagavad Gita

The design of the temple depends on symmetry.
Vitruvius

Sacred ground plans reflect balance and symmetry, representing the inexhaustible source, the world navel. Circles establish the sacred ground plans of a Hopi kiva (right) and the Roman Pantheon (far right).

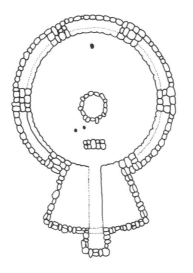
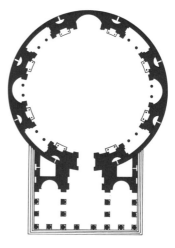

A temple is often built on the ground where an individual has come to this state of realization—a sacred structure that signifies and inspires the miracle of perfect centeredness, the place of break-through. The architecture of these holy places is defined by a sacred ground plan and cosmic house. These archetypal patterns of building translate the Upanishad's description of wholeness into a concrete place of dwelling. They shape the surroundings into a totality that nourishes mind, body, and nature.

The sacred ground plan reflects the inner harmony of balance and symmetry. It is usually shaped into forms of equilibrium—the square, rectangle, octagon, or circle. Like the eight-petaled lotus, the sacred ground plan offers a microcosm of time and space. It indicates the four directions—north, south, east, and west—and the inter-mediate points at the four corners. A shrine or altar at the center of the plan symbolizes the inexhaustible source, the world navel. In Navajo healing rites, the patient sits at the center of a circular, mythological sand painting in order to identify himself with its re-newing power. The Buddhist stupa at Borobudur is based on a man-dalalike series of concentric squares and circles that culminate in a bell-shaped structure that houses a statue of Buddha. Sacred archi-tecture in every region of the globe is built on these principles—the temples of Egypt, Greece, India, China, Japan, and ancient Mexico; the churches of Europe and North America; Islamic mosques; and Native American kivas, tepees, and hogans, to name a few. As a lotus

Concentric squares and circles form the mandalalike ground plan of the stupa at Borobudur, Java.

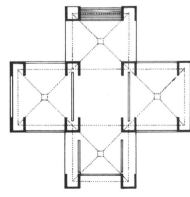

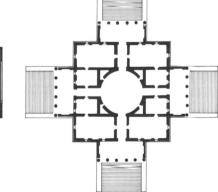

The square shapes the lotus seats of the Trenton Bath House by Louis Kahn (far left) and the Villa Capra by Andrea Palladio (left).

The Haida house was seen by the Native Americans of the Northwest coast as occupying the center of the universe, which they divided into three realms—underworld, earth, and sky. Each soul emerged from the underworld of the sea and dwelt in the house during its human existence.

At death the body was buried near the forest, which was associated with the sky realm.

The Pima of the American Southwest employed the archetypal elements of the cosmic house in their winter shelters, or ki, creating microcosms of universal design. A circle of holes dug into the earth imitated the horizon that rims human perception. Four posts connected by crossbeams defined the primal architectural form. A dome of willow poles echoed the endless canopy of the sky.

rooted in the mud reaches to open its petals to the sun, sacred ground plans are often raised on bases or steps that touch the earth while opening to the expanse of the sky. Greek temples, for example, were frequently placed on craggy mountaintops and gracefully lifted toward the heavens on a plinth of three steps. Many ancient cities were organized as sacred ground plans. They acted as lotus seats of collective consciousness, where the radiating spokes of goods and people could converge at the hub of community. The Book of Revelation describes the Heavenly Jerusalem as having a square plan with three gates on each of its four sides.

The sacred ground plan rises into the three-dimensional enclosure of the cosmic house. The two-dimensional wholeness of the sacred ground plan grows to symbolically envelop the totality of time and space. The Buddha's Immovable Spot was marked by the trunk and spreading branches of the bo tree. Four pillars and a roof create a basic architectural definition of the cosmic house. This primal structure emphasizes the four directions of north, south, east, and west while also pointing to the vertical dimensions of above and below. Churches, synagogues, mosques, temples, and Hopi kivas are all elaborations of this archetypal dwelling of consciousness. Jewish

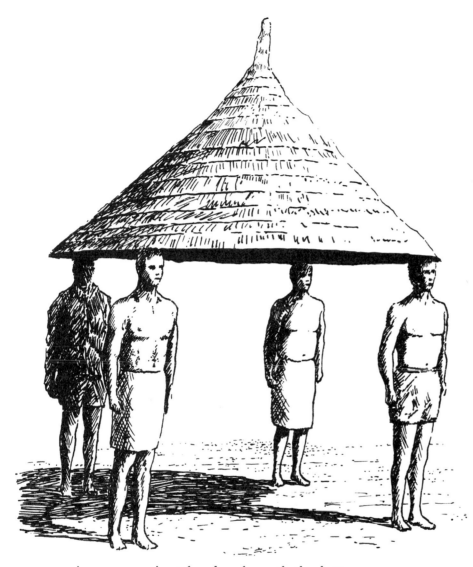

Guinea tribesmen form the primal expression of the cosmic dwelling—four posts and a canopy—as they move the roof of this house.

My dwellings are round, representing the universal circle of the nations' continuity. Our ancient dwellings are of earth, water, stone, wood, bark, and hide. I construct them as my ancestors did before me, with regard to the four directions, the rising sun, landmarks, tribal migrations. . . . The heart of each dwelling is a glow fire.
Anna Lee Walters

marriage ceremonies take place beneath the *huppa*, a canopy supported by four poles. Entering the cosmic house reenacts the universal pattern of returning to the source, reconnecting with the springs of eternal life, and then spreading those energies of renewal in the world. It silently reminds us that each life can pass through the gates of duality, travel the path of knowledge, and come to the lotus seat of fulfillment. The fullness of this experience is gained by thoroughly exploring the many implications of the cosmic house. The remaining chapters explore the ramifications of this idea.

A few sticks and leaves humbly define a minimal Indian temple where a sacred lingam resides.

You employ stone, wood, and concrete, and with these materials you build houses and palaces. . . . But suddenly you touch my heart. . . . That is Architecture.
Le Corbusier

Tu Lo Temple provides a cosmic house for the embodiment of compassion, the Chinese goddess Kuan-yin.

Seeing and Creating

1. Find the components of the gate described in this chapter at the entry to your home—approach, twin pillars, crossbeam, door, latch, key, hinge, and threshold. Notice how each element shapes the experience of passing through it. Imagine how you might alter the entry's design to enhance its sacredness. How could anticipation be heightened in the approach? Could the molding on either side of the door be painted in some way to strengthen the feeling of passing between twin pillars? Call out the crossbeam by hanging a wreath or draping material over the door. Notice the gateways you encounter in a day—at the office, bank, restaurant, grocery store, parking garage, and others. Perceive the numerous ways that the basic elements—approach, twin pillars, crossbeam, door, and threshold—are used. Imagine how they might be altered to evoke a greater sense of the sacred.

2. Witness how your consciousness changes as you pass through your house. Imagine how this journey could be enriched. Perhaps the ceiling height or color and texture of the walls might change as you moved through the spaces. Objects that hold special meaning for you could be placed along the way. Think of how the floor's material and color could reflect the transformations in consciousness you experience at each change in the path.

3. Notice the paths you traverse on a typical day—leaving home, going to work or school, engaging in some form of recreation. Be mindful of the connections between the qualities of thought and feeling you have and the changing architecture of the path. How might these paths be redesigned to reveal the mythic dimensions of your journey?

4. Locate the lotus seats, the places of arrival in your home—a comfortable chair, the dining room table, a bay window, the bed, etc. Experience the transition in your feelings that occurs when you go from a state of movement to a place of rest. See what architectural elements are used to define these places. Is there a lamp by the chair, a chandelier over the table, or a canopy over the bed? Find other lotus seats where you pause on a typical day—the chair at your desk, a bench in the park, the booth in a restaurant, the shelter of a bus stop.

THREE

Steeple and Sanctuary

Heaven is high, the earth is low; thus the Creative and the Receptive are determined. In correspondence with this difference between low and high, inferior and superior places are established.

Movement and rest have their definite laws; according to these, firm and yielding lines are differentiated.

Events follow definite trends, each according to its nature. Things are distinguished from one another in definite classes. In this way, good fortune and misfortune come about. In the heavens, phenomena take form; on earth, shapes take form. In this way, change and transformation become manifest.   **I CHING**

Gate, path, and lotus seat reflect the pattern of desire, search, and fulfillment. A second pattern—reaching outward for a higher level of life coupled with the inspiration of turning inward for healing and renewal—is reflected in the steeple and sanctuary. The steeple calls the mind to grow in knowledge and experience. Simultaneously, we are drawn to the qualities of the sanctuary—shelter, nurturing, stability, and loving embrace. The energies of steeple and sanctuary vivify the life of almost every building. Church spires, grain silos, water towers, skyscrapers, and other vertical shapes rise on the aspirations that strive to forge, in the words of Tom Robbins, "rods for psychic lightning and moorings for the Milky Way." The sheltering walls of each home, schoolhouse, church, and meeting hall hold the potential to be, as he says, "a chalice to cup the juices of existence and a womb for the ignition of the soul." If natural expansion is frustrated or distorted, it turns into the architecture of anger and aggression seen in guard towers and missile launchers. When gathering invokes the contractions of fear and isolation, it spawns the designs of walled cities and security-encircled apartment buildings. The eternal partners in the cosmic dance—male/female, yin/yang, light/dark, heaven/earth—are embodied in vertical and gathering forms. Such dualities appear everywhere that thought is given architectural shape: the roof peak that points to the star fields while you dream within the walls of your bedroom; the office tower that marks the rungs of the corporate ladder as it contains the human sparks of economic vitality; the monumental highway sign of a fast-food joint and the plastic-covered interior of its burger shrine.

STEEPLE

The steeple embodies the principles of the masculine, the organizing center, the outward journey, the urge to grow, and eternity breaking into the realm of time. Steeples of diverse shapes and sizes project these patterns of thought and feeling into three archetypal forms: axial pillars, sky doors, and world mountains.

The Achilpa of Australia tell the story of the divine being Numbakula, who made a sacred pole from a gum tree. After anointing it with blood, he climbed the pole and disappeared into the sky. This pole became the tribe's axial pillar, the hub of the revolving world. As the Achilpa journey across the land, they always carry their sacred pole with them, choosing their path by observing the direction toward which the pole bends. If the sacred pole breaks, their world plunges into chaos. After one such breakage, clan members wandered aimlessly until they finally lay down on the ground and waited for death to arrive. Without their vital centering device they had no means of communicating with the sky realm, their source of birth and renewal. A similar theme is depicted in the account of Moses leading the Israelites to the Promised Land. Their journey was guided by a pillar of cloud by day and a pillar of fire by night.

Axial pillars mark centers of psychic power and energy. The towering spire of the Washington Monument stands at the midpoint of the cross formed by the Capitol, Lincoln Memorial, White House, and Jefferson Memorial. It recalls the shape of an Egyptian obelisk, symbolically connecting the mythic "father of our country" with the

Cleave a piece of wood, I am there; lift up the stone and you will find me there.
The Thomas Gospel

A tall steeple [and] a rose window are not designed to allow additional seating or better light for reading. They speak to the soul's need for beauty, for love of the building itself as well as its use, for a special opportunity for sacred imagination.
Thomas Moore

A Native American embodies the aspirations of the steeple by holding aloft the mouthpiece of a sacred pipe as an offering to the great spirit above. He then sends puffs of smoke to the four directions. At his feet, a buffalo skull stands as a symbol of the sacrifice of life to life, of the compact between humans and nature. An offering of two decorated eagle feathers— one black, one white— has been placed between the horns, representing the dualities of existence: high and low, light and dark, life and death.

ancient wellsprings of Western civilization. A real Egyptian obelisk was dragged from its homeland and placed at the center of St. Peter's Square in Rome, marking the Catholic world's spiritual hub. An elaborate central pillar supports the vaulted ceiling of the Chapter House at Westminster Abbey, where the first English Parliament gathered. The Kwakiutl of British Columbia say that a copper pole, manifesting itself as the Milky Way, connects the underworld, earth, and sky. The massive trunk of a cedar tree, more than thirty feet tall, evokes this mythic image in the Kwakiutl ceremonial house. During the initiation ceremonies that take place there, the participants declare, "I am the Center of the World. . . . I am at the Post of the World." Using a tree—a universal symbol for regeneration—as an axial pillar intensifies the power of their sacred structure. Rising on the power of this primal concept, steeples of every shape and size radiate the qualities of vitality, youth, immortality, and knowledge to their surroundings. Minarets broadcast the call for prayer; clock towers measure the rhythms of living; lighthouses flash guiding rays of light; skyscrapers mark economic power points.

An obelisk is the focal point of St. Peter's Square in Rome. Notice how all of the design elements—the pattern of the piazza, the pillars, the statues atop the colonnade, and the boulevard—are organized by the axial pillar.

Axial pillars such as these stand at the center of English chapter houses. The ribbed vaults that support the roof are gathered and supported by the central post, echoing the structure of a society where individuals gather together for the purposes of mutual support.

A Los Angeles clothing store invites customers to converge on its entry with an axial pillar.

The walled enclosure of St. Katherine's Convent on Mount Sinai is entered by way of a rope lowered from above.

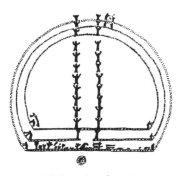

A Polynesian drawing shows the first humans rising through a sky door to shape the universe.

The ladder of a Hopi kiva connects earth and sky.

The sky door offers another means for heart and mind to ride the rising energies of the spirit. It takes the form of a central roof opening that connects a building to the sky's dynamic freedom by allowing solar rays to ignite human aspiration. The image of a ladder let down through an opening in midsky—as if through a golden sun door to the navel of the earth—is a universal mythic prototype. The Old Testament describes this motif in Jacob's dream: "And he dreamed, and behold a ladder set up on the earth, and the top of it reached to heaven: and behold the angels of God ascending and descending on it." The shamans of central Asia are said to climb up a ladder of consciousness to heaven through a hole in the cone-shaped roofs of their yurts. Native Americans used sky doors in diverse settings across the continent. It was felt that this architectural device allowed the human spirit to be lifted on ascending smoke from the hub of earthly existence to the hub of the celestial wheel that unites and turns the upper and lower worlds. The power of this idea strikes anyone who enters the Pantheon in Rome, where a thick shaft of light pours through an oculus at the pinnacle of the immense dome. Skylights in the living room of a home and the atriums of office buildings that bring in light from above echo this primal design concept.

Consider the honeybee, which first buzzes loudly while circling a flower, but finally settles in deep silence with the core of the fragrant blossom. This is the portal to samadhi.
Ramakrishna

The sky door of the Creative Artists Agency by Pei Cobb Freed & Partners (right) connects earthly concerns with the rhythms of the sun, moon, and stars and recalls the ancient Pantheon in Rome (lower right).

The energies of the axial pillar and sky door support the mythic image of the world mountain—the mass of experience one ascends during spiritual transformation. Since it connects heaven and earth, the world mountain stands at the psychic center of the cosmos. It is the fountainhead of all creative and renewing energies, the source of order and harmony in a chaotic world. The stepped towers of the Mayans and Aztecs in pre-Columbian America clothed this underlying notion in a distinct outer form. In Java the shape of the enormous temple of Borobudur is meant to imitate a passage from the confusion of the profane world, through stage after stage of awakening, to a breakthrough into the "pure region" of the transcendent.

The stupa at Borobudur rises in the mythic image of the world mountain. The terraces touching the earth at its base are square, facing the four directions. Those near the summit are circular, imitating the unbroken wholeness of heaven. At the pinnacle, the stupa's mass narrows, suggesting a vertical passage from the physical world to the transcendence of unlimited space.

The skyline of most modern cities reflects the notion of the world mountain—building masses clustered together and rising higher and higher toward the center. Many Victorian houses are based on this idea, with gable after gable piled one on top of the other toward the pinnacle. The apartment buildings constructed in New York City in the 1930s and 1940s step skyward in zigguratlike fashion, creating mountainous architectural forms.

An African mosque (right) and the Chrysler Building in New York (opposite) rise on the energies of the world mountain.

An Egyptian drawing from about 1000 B.C. depicts the separation of heaven and earth as the sky-goddess Nut arching over the reclining figure of her husband, the earth-god Geb. Nut's body, adorned with stars, is supported by the standing, pillarlike figure of the air-god Shu.

The stages of the mind's spiritual ascent as depicted in a Tibetan temple banner (opposite, left) are reflected in a Nepalese stupa (opposite, right); a Chinese temple (left); and a Native American tepee (above).

The steeple forms of axial pillar, sky door, and world mountain each incorporate the three-part structure of base, middle, and top, repeating the primal pattern of gate, path, and lotus seat in the vertical dimension. The base is rooted in the depths of the soil—diversity, materiality, and the directions of the four-square earth dominate. The middle indicates movement in the mundane world and the graded stages of development during spiritual ascent. The top narrows in ever-finer lines that disappear into the transcendence of the sky, pointing toward oneness and nonmaterial spirit. Buddhist stupas convey this idea by stacking five geometric forms on top of one another: square, circle, triangle, crescent, and diamond. Each form is related to a different quality of density. The square at the base symbolizes the most compact state, earth; the circle equals water; the triangle equals fire; the crescent equals air; and the diamond represents the ethereal qualities of space.

The five geometric forms of a Buddhist stupa represent, from the bottom, the elements of earth, water, fire, air, and space.

63

SANCTUARY

The sanctuary balances and integrates the energies of the steeple. Where the steeple expresses the polarities of earth and sky, dark and light, and the wounding of the psyche caused by separation from our true nature, the sanctuary represents the joining together of these energies. It echoes the words of Krishna spoken on the field of dharma:

I am the Self, seated in the heart of all creatures. I am the beginning, middle, and the end. . . .

The sanctuary offers a place for healing the rifts between body and mind—a safe harbor for shedding worn-out modes of experience. It embodies the inward turn of consciousness, the cave, the feminine, the cosmic egg. These ideas are given physical reality through the architectural devices of the portal, central aisle, and altar.

The portal, like the gate described in Chapter Two, signals the transition from the chaos of the outer world to the peace of the inner one. Employing the components of the gate—the approach, twin pillars, crossbeam, door, latch, key, hinge, and threshold—the portal marks the first step in the healing of the psyche. Entering the portal—like Jonah being swallowed by the whale—marks the beginning of a new spiritual existence. In the Pacific Northwest, the Kwakiutl expressed this by constructing the doorways of their houses in the form of huge bird beaks. Passing through the portal of a large hospital, government building, or corporation can also feel like a devouring. Once ingested through the "mouth" of these institutions, we pass through a labyrinth of rooms and bureaucratic procedures until we are "spit out" onto the street.

The central aisle passing through the middle of the sanctuary marks the passage to enlightenment, the process of healing. Lining the central aisles of many sanctuaries, pillars imitate the rhythmic pulsations of time, ticking off the progression of restoration and awakening. Those on the interior of Vézelay Cathedral depict time with carved scenes of the seasonal activities of planting, cultivating, and harvesting. Paradoxically, time touches the timeless in the middle of the sanctuary. To the sides of the central aisle are places to sit in subdued light. Mind and body can become absorbed in silence and wholeness, pausing in the stillness before taking the next steps of the journey toward the altar.

The beak of the snapping door on a Vancouver Island ceremonial house clearly expresses the warning that only worthy people can enter unharmed. It is lowered during ritual occasions, providing an entry ramp for guests to climb through its throat (opposite).

The doorway of a palazzo in Rome actually "swallows" visitors.

The central aisle of Vézelay Cathedral indicates the path of the sacred. It passes through the middle of the sanctuary and conveys the mythic image of the belly of the whale—the place where consciousness turns inward to rediscover the self (right).
The Chicago O'Hare United Airlines Terminal is a modern example of the central aisle idea (opposite).

The archetype of the central aisle is the guiding design principle of Chicago's O'Hare United Airlines Terminal by Murphy/Jahn Architects. Glass-covered arcades link passenger check-in, waiting lounges, boarding gates, and baggage claim. Passengers can move rapidly along the central aisle of the arcade or rest in the side "chapels" of the waiting lounges. The rhythms of day and night can be followed through the glass enclosure. Clocks and information monitors at regular intervals along the central aisle orchestrate the flow of traffic.

The pillars on the interior of Vézelay Cathedral depict time by showing the seasonal activities of planting, cultivating, and harvesting (opposite). The pillars lining the central aisle of Sant'Apollinare Nuovo imitate the rhythmic pulsations of time and the process of inner transformation. The mosaic figures on the frieze above the colonnade reinforce this idea (left).

Using a form similar to that of a church or temple, arrival and departure gates gather around the altarlike apse of the Chicago O'Hare United Airlines Terminal.

Sacred stones often serve as altars. Like a seed within the enclosing pod of a sanctuary, a sacred stone provides a center from which the individual and the cosmos are symbolically regenerated.

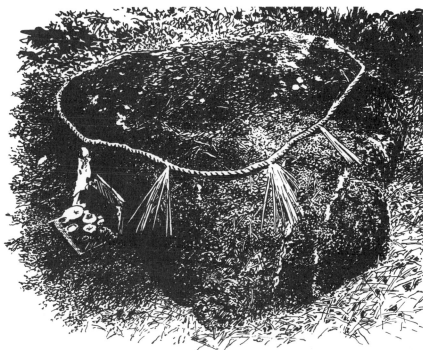

Every life needs its altar. It may be in a church or quiet nook, it may be a moment in the day, or a mood of the heart . . . but somewhere the spiritual life must have its altar. From there, life gains its poise and direction.
Esther B. York

71

The altar signals the place of arrival and rebirth. It is the focal point of the sanctuary; the seed within the pod of its enclosing floor, walls, and roof; the world navel. According to the Rig Veda, the universe sprouts from a central umbilical point and spreads in all directions. It is depicted by the image of Brahma, the creator, sitting on a lotus growing from the navel of the sleeping Vishnu. The Sama Veda describes the arrival at the altar of self-realization by declaring, "You are there! You are there! What was far away is now near. Light is dawning in all directions into its own source." Hebrew thought is very precise on this point:

> The Most Holy One created the world like an embryo. As the Embryo grows from the navel, so God began to create the world by the navel and from there it spread in all directions.

The sacred stone housed within the Dome of the Rock in Jerusalem is called "the Foundation Stone of the Earth" by the Jews,

Art is the path of the creator to his work.
Emerson

Inside my empty bottle I was constructing a lighthouse while others were making ships.
C. S. Lewis

The curving form of an apse draws attention to the altars of an Italian church (right) and an Indian cave temple (opposite).

because it is from this place that their world unfolded. Islamic tradition draws on a similar image. Five times a day Muslims orient their prayers to the holy city of Mecca, which is built around the Kaaba, the stone placed there by Abraham as an outward sign of his inner transformation. During the setting of the stone, he said, "That stone I set here as a memory of initiation . . . that this stone shall remain forever as a temple." In Japanese gardens such as Ryoan-ji, stones serve as focal points for contemplation.

Because the altar serves as the power point for regeneration, it is usually raised or lowered in relation to its surroundings. When lowered, it represents the open womb from which creation springs. A raised altar suggests the swelling of seed energies sprouting into diverse expressions. Often this part of the sanctuary is defined by a semicircular wall called an apse. The enclosing space takes on the role of the open womb; the raised altar is the germinating inner force. Light is greatest here. Coming from east-facing windows or groupings of candles, it energizes the renewing ritual.

Gardens are constructions of time. Rocks hardly change at all, they are a stable presence. But plants change with the seasons, they come and go. I try to work these elements into an orchestra, parts that change quickly, others that don't change at all. Enveloping it all is the earth and the sky; and sometimes it rains. So really what I do is I design gardens with music.
Toru Takemitsu

Beauty is that which has been liberated from duality.
Soetsu Yanagi

The archetype of steeple and sanctuary inform the design of a Victorian house (opposite), and a county courthouse (left).

A manifestation of the Sacred is always a revelation of Being.
Mircea Eliade

With a cluster of steeple and sanctuary forms, this contemporary Midwest home shelters a family's needs and encourages the expansion of its dreams.

At each point in our environment, the archetypes of steeple and sanctuary are clothed in forms that respond to the needs of a particular place. A skyscraper provides a center for office workers; a minaret, a focal point for prayer. A bus stop offers shelter from the elements; a restaurant, a nourishing haven; an automobile, a private sanctum among a river of commuters. Every inflection of the steeple and sanctuary acts as a centering device that reestablishes harmonious patterns in an apparently chaotic world. The energies that are depleted and the wounds that are created by the comings and goings of living are replenished and healed at these points of architectural balance. The eight elemental building blocks that compose steeples and sanctuaries are discussed in the next chapter.

Seeing and Creating

1. Look for ways your home expresses the three qualities of the steeple: axial pillar, sky door, and world mountain. Is there a central chimney or column that embodies the axial pillar? The sky door might be found at a stairway that rises through an opening between floors, in a skylight, or in a window placed high on a wall. See if the exterior of your house reflects the qualities of the world mountain by rising from a wider base to a narrower pinnacle.

2. Imagine how you might enhance the qualities of the steeple in your home. Could a tree or fountain be placed at the center of your garden to create an axial pillar? Where could you place a skylight to enjoy the qualities of a sky door? How might you paint the exterior of your house, or add a roof ornament, to enhance the qualities of a world mountain?

3. Notice how the axial pillar, sky door, and world mountain take shape in the architecture of your community. Is there a tall building that creates an axial pillar at the center of the business district or a university campus? Pause for a moment to experience the qualities of consciousness it embodies. Find a building that has a skylit atrium in order to experience the qualities of a sky door; see how the connection to the sky that it provides alters the feeling of the place. Look for a building or group of buildings that steps up toward a pinnacle to reflect the characteristics of the world mountain; experience the change in your consciousness as your perception rises from the solid mass of the building's base along its contours to the highest point touching the sky.

4. See if you can find the three architectural components of a sanctuary—portal, central aisle, and altar—in an unlikely place. In a supermarket, fruit and other items are often displayed in altarlike forms at the end of a long aisle. Pause for a moment and feel the qualities of healing and renewal that may be offered. Look for ways this pattern is embedded in other buildings such as banks and post offices.

5. Think of how you could transform a room in your house to become more like a sanctuary. How would you design the doorway to exhibit the qualities of the portal? Could the furniture, rugs, or other elements be arranged to shape a central aisle? Design an altar for this room.

The Eight Elemental Forms

I used to worship the Deity at the Kali Temple. It was suddenly revealed to me that everything is Pure Spirit. The utensils of worship, the altar, the door frame—all Pure Spirit. Men, animals, and other living beings—all Pure Spirit. Like a madman I began to shower flowers in all directions. Whatever I saw I worshipped. **RAMAKRISHNA**
Ritual Art of India

Gate, path, and lotus seat as well as steeple and sanctuary are holistic organizing principles in architecture. They mold a building into patterns that integrate mind and surroundings. Just as overall architectural form has direct connections to the workings of consciousness, the individual parts—such as walls and roofs—also serve as links between spirit and matter. Each piece of a building has a corresponding form of thought and feeling. Eight fundamental forms give every building—from the tent of a nomadic tribesman to a Manhattan skyscraper—its structure. They consist of: floors, walls, pillars, roofs, space, doors and windows, ornament, and rooms—eight elemental forms that make up architecture's basic alphabet.

These eight archetypal forms are clothed in different styles by the people who use them. Architecture in every time and place has a floor, for example. Whether this archetype takes on the character of a Kentucky barn's dirt floor or an English palace's marble one depends on the information that is expressed through that form. By receiving and reflecting the information we feed into them, these eight archetypal building elements become tangible connectors to the sacred.

FLOOR

The floor beneath your feet embodies the desire to find stable ground in a world of constant flux. Level and firm, it externalizes the consciousness of support and uplift, acting as a spreading field of information that gives walls and pillars a place to stand. The floor is a stage, the unmoving, eternal base upon which the diverse play of life is enacted. When we make a floor, we engage in the primal act of marking the boundaries of our personal territory. Drawing lines on the spreading earth establishes our home in the world.

Lines drawn on an Iowa prairie define a homestead and surrounding farms.

    The simple act of spreading a picnic blanket on a lawn provides a glimpse of a floor's power. This rectangular piece of cloth does far more than protect us from the dirt and the dew; it defines a zone within nature's continuum that will act as the center for the day's activities. Gathering with friends, playing a game of softball, and exploring in the woods all refer back to this spot that has been marked for the day with a mere piece of cloth.

    Wherever our minds and bodies touch the physical environment, this archetype takes on a specific outer form that precisely reflects an inner pattern of consciousness. The thoughts and actions of eating a meal transform the floor archetype into the level and firm surfaces of a tabletop, chair seats, and dinner plates. The desire to move from the first floor to the second collects a series of small floors together into the rising increments that create a flight of stairs. With the intention to display a photograph, a vase, or some books, the floor becomes a shelf. A kitchen countertop is the result of mixing the idea of a floor with information about chopping and preparing food.

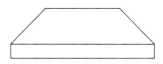
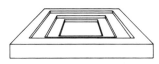

Three types of floor: raised, level, lowered.

The floor archetype can be raised or lowered to express the inner feeling of expansion or contraction. As previously mentioned, Greek temples were lifted toward the heavens by placing them atop craggy hills. The actual floor of these temples was raised above the surrounding ground on a plinth of three steps. The act of climbing from the floor of a valley to one of these sacred places mirrored the ascension of the spirit. Greek amphitheaters, on the other hand, employed a series of lowered, bowl-shaped floor planes to create a sense of gathering and community. Where the temple on the hill rose to a unique point of singularity, the amphitheater drew diverse people together in an experience of communal unity. Raising or lowering any floor encourages these experiences in consciousness. A vase set on a pedestal calls attention to a unique object worthy of praise. The lowered floor of a sunken living room reinforces the gathering energies of cradling and security that are essential to family life.

The visible world was made to correspond to the world invisible and there is nothing in this world but is a symbol of something in that other world.
al-Ghazali

The steps at the apse of Santa Maria Maggiore in Rome (1673), by Carlo Rainaldi, connect the floor level of the church to that of the Piazza dell'Esquilino.

81

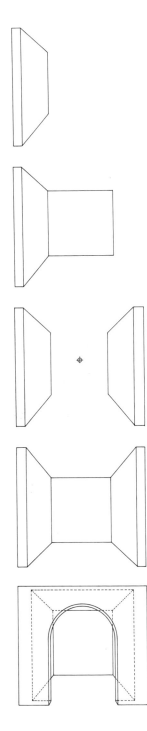

WALL

Rising from the floor is the archetype of the wall, expressing the consciousness of separation and enclosure. This fundamental building element distinguishes inside from out and separates floors from roofs to create habitable spaces. The rising energies of exterior walls temper the sun's light and protect us from wind and rain. They are shaped to cradle us in security and simultaneously urge us out into the world. Acting as so many masks veiling the play of interior life, building facades both hide and reveal the secrets of their inner realms.

A single wall is a layer of information that cuts one space into two. It provides a reference point for organizing our surroundings in ways that comfort and protect us. We experience the nurturing presence of a single wall while sitting on a porch with our backs against a house. Our perception expands away from the single upright surface behind us as we look out at the world. It contracts toward the wall as we lean into the stable reference point of the home. As the need arises, this archetype takes on other inflections of verticality, such as bookcases, chair backs, and garden hedges.

The size and proportion of walls shape our experiences of dwelling. The back of a chair can comfortably harmonize with the size of our own backs or can stand formally above us. We feel tall in relation to a knee-high garden hedge and dwarfed by one that towers overhead. The twenty-foot walls of a double-height living room urge our perceptions to expand along the soaring verticality of their surfaces.

Memories of earlier times and hopes for the future are also deposited in walls. As they surround our bodies they define the spaces within our minds. A cabinet full of toys marks the edges of a child's world. Castles gain their wondrous qualities from the massive walls that surround them. Gleaming white masonry walls on a Greek isle, dense hedgerows in the English countryside, or split-rail fences in the Rocky Mountains trigger diverse worlds of associations within us. The Great Wall of China embodies the collective consciousness of the nation that built it. The Wailing Wall in Jerusalem is an ancient piece of the enclosure of Herod's temple near the Holy of Holies; for millions of Jews it is a sacred place for prayer and purification, a source of comfort and consolation.

Two or more walls working together can provide numerous qualities of spatial experience. Parallel wall planes, such as those in a hallway, guide our attention along their length to the open spaces at their ends. Joining a pair of walls together to form a corner gives us the first consciousness of interior and exterior space. Interior corners tend to gather, or contract, our awareness, while exterior corners tend to expand it into the surroundings. Three walls can be arranged to make a U-shaped enclosure and focus consciousness toward a specific area. The interiors of bay windows, niches, alcoves, and other recessed enclosures provide harbors for mind and body. Four or more vertical planes complete the idea of enclosure, making a definite distinction between the consciousness of interior and exterior.

PILLAR

Of the eight archetypal building elements, pillars are our closest kin. As tangible expressions of the creative energies within us, they are physical embodiments of hope and strength. Imitating our stance on the landscape, pillars echo the proportions of our height and slenderness. Meeting the floor, they spread out in floorlike supports. Legs and torsos are reflected in a pillar's shaft, while our heads are imitated by their capitals. As we rise to overcome the force of gravity, pillars stand beside us. The ancient Greeks beautifully expressed the kinship of consciousness and matter at the Erechtheion in Athens, where six pillars, carved in the shape of women, form the southern portico of the temple, displaying a direct relationship between the spirit that informs human life and architecture.

There is a map of the universe in the lines that time draws on these old walls.
Gaston Bachelard

And Jacob . . . took the stone that he had put for his pillow, and set it up for a pillar, and poured oil upon the top of it. And he called the name of that place Beth-el [the House of God].
Genesis

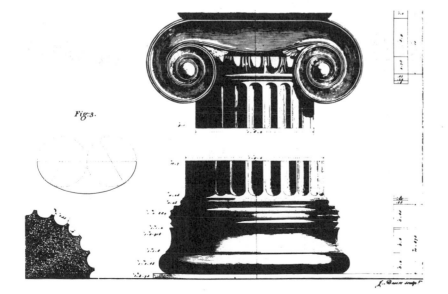

Fig. 3.

The design of this Ionic column expresses the structural forces at work within it. Spiraling volutes at the top spread under the weight of the beam. The base becomes a rolling bulge where the heft of the column meets the floor.

83

Pillars can also display the structural forces working within them. In classical columns the powerful energies of pressing down and squeezing out that occur at the point where the column's shaft meets the floor are expressed in the rolling bulges of the base. The shaft swells with the forces working at its core to resist gravity's pull. The capital spreads in response to the weight of the beam it supports. This timeless way of shaping pillars echoes the psychological and physical forces within us. After standing or walking for long periods of time, our feet swell. Carrying a heavy load, the muscles of our legs and torsos expand. Taking on the weight of extra obligations is called "shouldering responsibility."

The pillars of the Erechtheion's caryatid porch in Athens show the kinship between pillars and human form (right). Pompey's Pillar in Alexandria is a monumental version of our own stance on the landscape (below).

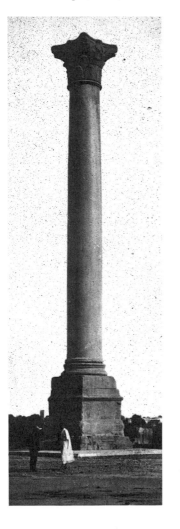

The dome of the Florence Cathedral spans the octagonal transept of the building, giving aspiration and faith a tangible form.

We . . . build our churches high, so that those who enter feel themselves elevated and the soul can rise to the contemplation of God.
Alberti

ROOF

Roofs spread out to provide shelter, echoing the endless dome of the sky. Rising in steeple forms, they create beacons on the horizon. Roofs shape interior ceilings that offer canopies for dreaming. As Michelangelo's Sistine Chapel displays, they become screens for projecting expansive aspirations. Bridging cavernous distances, roofs symbolize monumental leaps of faith. The original architect of the Florence Cathedral planned to have a huge dome covering the building's octagonal transept, even though he lacked the technology to achieve such a feat. He believed that someone would expand the repertoire of possibilities, so construction began in 1296. The day came when the entire structure was complete except for the dome of faith. The cathedral remained uncovered until 1420, when Filippo Brunelleschi designed a unique double-shelled dome.

The stone and wood construction bears the same relation to architecture as the piano does to the music played upon it. Architecture and music are the conveyors of expression of human experience.
Bernard Maybeck

Delicate ribwork at Chartres Cathedral transforms tons of stone into an airy ceiling (right). At a mosque in Damascus, coffers and a lantern allow a massive dome to dematerialize into light (lower right).

The space within the building is the reality of that building.
Frank Lloyd Wright

SPACE

Floors, walls, pillars, and roofs join forces to shape habitable space, the elusive archetype that offers up the ultimate mystery: "From the nothing the begetting, from the nothing the increase, from the nothing the abundance," declare the Upanishads. Space is not created by architecture, but is revealed by it. The twin pillars and crossbeam of a Japanese gateway, for example, capture a piece of space, orienting our attention to the passageway. Of all architectural elements, space

*I enjoy the silence in a church
before the service
more than any sermon.*
Emerson

*At Chartres Cathedral, a row
of piers and pointed arches
compresses the space of a side
aisle, serving as a foil to the
soaring space of the
central aisle on the left.*

87

most directly displays the qualities of consciousness; like pure awareness, it has no tangible attributes, but takes on the characteristics of
the environment it inhabits. Although it is nonphysical, it is the center of all physical pursuits. The Tao te Ching explains:

> We join spokes of a wheel, but it is the center hole that makes
> the wagon move.
> We shape clay into a pot, but it is the emptiness inside that
> holds whatever we want.
> We hammer wood for a house, but it is the inner space that
> makes it livable.

The spiritual qualities of sacred places are largely a matter of the
shape they give to space. Space is the unseen connector of all things,
the invisible gap that unites the visible elements of architecture.

Within the limitlessness of space we become aware of the desire
to make the sacred places of our lives. A bit of space is scooped from
the vast expanse of the world, providing a place for the human spirit
to reside. Space is then shaped in ways that respond to patterns of
thought and feeling. The consciousness of moving from one place to
another informs the space of a hallway, for example. Every thought
we have and action we perform shapes space in some way, giving it
specific qualities.

DOORS AND WINDOWS

While floors, walls, and roofs define and protect our dwelling places,
doors and windows allow the nourishing influences of sunlight, air,
food, and friendship to bring them to life. In the same way that vital
information passes through the openings of our eyes, ears, nose, and
mouth, architecture touches the surroundings through the openings
of windows and doors—places where our private lives and the universe overlap. This overlapping of a building's inner and outer worlds
is altered by the character of the openings we create. Varying the size,
shape, position, and material of a window or door determines the
quantity and quality of the information that enters our consciousness. The world we perceive through picture window overlooking a
garden is very different from the one we experience through a tiny
circle of stained glass placed near the peak of a vaulted ceiling.

Doors and windows are tools for expressing the consciousness of

*The object of any creative
effort in the visual arts is to
give form to space. But what is
space, how can it be understood
and given form?*
Walter Gropius

*But he alone gains
[enlightenment] who knows its
doors; for what were he to do
with a house who cannot find
his way inside.*
Satapatha Brahmana

*God is the home of the
soul, just as space is the home
of the body.*
Alfred A. Montapert

a building. They give character to our dwellings and hold out the life within as an offering to the rest of society. Our eyes are the "windows of the soul"; the gaps we fashion in the walls of our living environments define how we relate to others of our kind.

The shape of a door or window serves as a storehouse of personal and cultural memory. An arched window can be vibrant with the cultural recollections of ancient Rome and the Italian Renaissance. By reshaping this opening into a pointed arch, the memory of medieval Europe is enlivened in our consciousness. The simple elegance of a tall, double-hung window recalls the one-room schoolhouses that grace America's heritage. Seeing a casement window with a flower-filled window box may stir remembrances of homes in the Swiss Alps. Adding ornate or formal trim to a doorway can awaken memories of the grand houses of England or France. The exquisitely simple joinery of a garden gate can bring our awareness to thoughts of Japan.

Sunlight, views, and breezes overlap with a living room through the doors and windows of a home designed by Lawlor/Weller Design Group.

*I think that a plan is
a society of rooms. A real
plan is one in which the rooms
have spoken to each other.*
Louis Kahn

*Go sweep out the chamber
of your heart. Make it ready
for the dwelling place
of the Beloved.*
Mahmud Shabistri

ORNAMENT

Architecture is created by joining building materials into a unified whole. At each point where one physical substance meets another, traces of the mind and body's handiwork are displayed. These points of joining are called ornament. As an expression of the meeting of consciousness and matter, ornament is an essential element in rendering architecture sacred. It is the tangible expression of the human spirit flowing into actions that shape the world.

Ornament can range from the simple meeting of a quiet awareness to a dazzling display of exuberant consciousness. The seat, legs, and back of a Shaker chair are joined with modest elegance; each part is connected to the other with a minimum of effort; a slight curve here, a peg there, express the subtle inflections of consciousness at work in crafting this piece of furniture. The interior of a Baroque church, by contrast, is a high-spirited gesture of complex virtuosity; in the flamboyantly decorated walls, pillars, and ceiling, layer upon layer of stone, plaster, and paint unite in a riotous dance; the revelations of heart and mind climb heavenward in an opulent display of architectural possibilities.

At the points where our consciousness joins the external stimuli of our surroundings, an ornament of the mind is created. When the sounds, textures, sights, tastes, and fragrances of a building or landscape pass through the senses to the mind, they are embellished by our personal ways of perceiving and interpretation. The ability to see the pillar of a Greek temple, for instance, involves a complex joining of mind, body, and environment. This process begins with light falling on a carved stone. When we look at it, the reflected light enters our eyes and stimulates an electrochemical reaction that sends this impression to the brain. This is interpreted as a specific pattern of light and shadow. Living in a Western culture, we learn to perceive this particular pattern of light and shadow as a classical column, which has something to do with the architectural components of a building. This perception is then given another layer of ornamentation by our past experience with this type of column. We may remember having seen this particular pattern of light and shadow on an imposing bank, library, or administration building. It may be filtered through memories of a vacation in Greece or a movie about the Roman Empire. In any case, a type of perceptual ornament is generated from the joining of consciousness and matter.

Ornament depicts unity in multiplicity. Like diverse people coming together to celebrate and renew the human spirit, architectural ornament joins brick and wood, stone and plaster in ways that glorify creation. As in Michelangelo's famous painting of the hand of God reaching to give life to Adam, the power of ornament resides in the touchpoints between materials. Here the energy and intelligence within us does its silent work—crafting the stuff of life into sacred forms. When spirit joins the matter of the world, architectural progeny are born.

*Ornament
is the adoration of the joint.*
Louis Kahn

*Architectural ornament is
created by honoring the
juncture of building elements.
Joining a beam and rafters to
a pillar generates the
construction of practical
embellishment.*

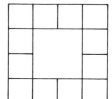

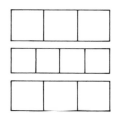

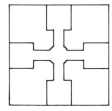

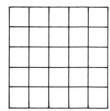

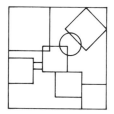

Five types of room organization: centralized, radial, linear, gridlike, and clustered.

ROOMS

The joining of floors, walls, pillars, roofs, space, doors and windows, and ornament finds significance in the creation of rooms. The thoughts and actions that transform raw materials into architectural elements find wholeness in a defined dwelling place. Here the attributes of mind, body, and architecture mingle with the seven archetypal building forms described above to create sacred places.

Two fundamental patterns of consciousness inform the design of rooms—patterns of path and patterns of place. Rooms of the path encourage the passage of mind and body through space. A hallway or stairway invites movement from one destination to another. Rooms of the place, on the other hand, tend to center our awareness on a particular spot. A room for sleeping focuses on the bed, while one for cooking revolves around cabinets, preparation surfaces, and a stove. Rooms of path and place can be distinctly separate or woven together to create multilayered experiences of rest and activity. A gallery combined with bookcases and a window seat can serve as both a place of passage and a place to linger.

Rooms can be arranged in five basic ways. *Centralized* organizations embody the movement of consciousness toward an inward, centered direction. *Radial* layouts externalize the outward expansion of awareness that spreads into the world while always referring to the core of existence. *Linear* rooms mirror the sequential unfolding of knowledge along the path of realization. Rooms arranged in a *grid* offer a glimpse of awareness that comprehends the totality of existence as well as each part. *Clustered* plans symbolize the desire to unify diverse qualities of experience. In any arrangement, rooms offer lotus seats, places where consciousness turns back on itself to heal and renew mind and body. How architecture integrates consciousness and physiology is the subject of the next chapter.

Rooms can support movement along a path or arrival at a place, reflecting the soul's tendencies to seek and to find.

*Every detail surrounding this
Paris window celebrates the art
of joining materials.
Oversized brackets support the
balcony with its
delicate iron railing.
Horizontal grooves delineate
courses of stone. The doorway's
crossbeam rises
in a graceful arch.*

*But the large rooms
ought to be related to the
middle ones, and these to
the small, that . . . one part
of the building may correspond
to the other, so that the whole
body of the edifice may
have itself a certain
harmony of members which
may make it entirely beautiful
and graceful.*
Andrea Palladio

Seeing and Creating

1. See how the floor archetype takes on various shapes and sizes. Does it become a table, seat of a chair, or a bookshelf? Become aware of how raising or lowering the floor affects the importance you give to the objects placed on it. How do the materials, textures, and colors of the floor vary as it takes on different shapes? Think of the ways that these horizontal surfaces could be redesigned to enhance their sacredness.

2. What are the qualities of enclosure displayed by the walls that surround you? Notice how chair backs, bookcases, screens, and other furniture create smaller walls. What materials, textures, colors, and shapes are used to reinforce the characteristics of enclosure? How might these be altered to change the feeling?

3. Notice any pillars in your setting; they might take the form of table legs, standing lamps, candlesticks, or other items. How might these be redesigned to imitate your own stance and aspirations?

4. Think of ways you could change the ceiling to inspire a more expansive experience or greater life and depth. Could fabric be used on a frame to give it the shape of a barrel vault or peak?

5. See how the floors, walls, pillars, and ceiling sculpt the space. How could the furniture be rearranged to squeeze the space or open it?

6. How do doors and windows affect the place? Think of the ways they allow life to flow in and out. What transitions in feeling take place at the doorways? How would altering their size, shape, and number change the experience? In what ways do the windows express the soul of the place? How might you reconfigure them to express a different quality of consciousness?

7. Notice how materials are joined to create ornament. What qualities of consciousness did the builders store in the ornament? Can you see their care, dullness, humor, or other qualities? What information might you add to keep this dialogue going?

8. Notice the arrangement of rooms in your house. Are they placed in a pattern that is centralized, radial, linear, gridlike, or clustered? Feel the qualities of consciousness that this floor plan encourages, such as orderliness, chaos, or integration.

Mind ▪ *Body* ▪ *Architecture*

Within the city of Brahman, which is the body, there is the heart, and within the heart there is a little house. This house has the shape of a lotus, and within it dwells that which is to be sought after, inquired about, and realized.

What then, is that which dwells within this house, the lotus of the heart? . . .

Even so large as the universe outside is the universe within the lotus of the heart. Within it are heaven and earth, the sun, the moon, the lightning, and all the stars. Whatever is in the macrocosm is in this microcosm. **CHANDOGYA UPANISHAD**

The mind's patterns of thinking are clothed by the body. Through the doorway of the body, inner thoughts pass to outer conditions and outer circumstances pass to inner experience. Architecture extends our human form into the physical structures we create. Walls and roofs act as a second "skin" that encloses our own skin. Buildings also reflect mental patterns of thinking and perceiving. As discussed in Chapter Three, a steeple can embody the tendencies of consciousness to expand into new realms of experience, while a sanctuary can be an outward expression of the desire for gathering and renewal. The word *facade*, used to denote the front of a building, has the same root as *face*. The doors and windows of many buildings are arranged in patterns that recall the eyes, nose, and mouth of the human face.

The men dressed as New York skyscrapers are the architects who designed the actual buildings (right). The tiled facade of San Miniato al Monte overlooks the city of Florence. Notice the lotus pattern at the "third eye" in the small arches above the "nose" and "eyes" of the design (below).

These northern Aranda tribesmen of Australia become living architecture in order to create a sacred place.

An Aztec legend puts the connections between body and environment in mythic terms. It describes how the gods Quetzalcoatl, the Plumed Serpent, and Tezcatlipoca, the Smoking Mirror, fashioned the world from the body of the goddess Tlalteutli. From her hair they made trees, flowers, and grass; from her eyes, springs, fountains, and little caves; from her nose, valleys; and from her shoulders, mountains. An Indian story relates how the universal spirit took the form of Purusha, the first person, and how the gods created the world by performing a sacrifice with Purusha's body. The sky rose from his head, the air from his navel, the earth from his feet, the moon from his mind, the sun from his eye, and the four quarters of space from his ear. An ancient Indian manual on architecture contains a drawing of Purusha's body pressed between the confines of a square diagram called the Vastu Purusha mandala.

There is only one temple in this world and that is the human body.
Novalis

99

This diagram was used as the fundamental pattern for almost every type of building in India—from the floor plans of simple huts to the layouts of entire cities. Purusha is also seen as the cosmic person within each individual; placing his body inside this archetypal floor plan represented the link between universal intelligence, individual consciousness, the human body, and the architecture that houses it. A Renaissance drawing by Francesco di Giorgio echoes this theme by showing the relationship between a human figure and a cathedral floor plan. Di Giorgio and other Renaissance thinkers reasoned that if humans were "made in the image of God," their physical form was the ideal model for creating architectural forms that reflected the divine.

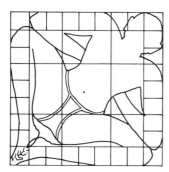

Vastu Purusha mandala.

Diverse cultures have related the body's form and function to environmental shapes and processes. The belly or womb was represented by a room, the intestines by a labyrinth, breathing by weaving, the veins and arteries by the sun and moon, the backbone by the central pillar, the heart or navel by the center of the world. A Vedic text refers to the body as "a house with a pillar and nine doors." The sky door placed at the top of many domes is called an "eye," or oculus. The upper opening of an Indian tower is called a *brahmarandhra*, a term that also designates the opening in the top of the skull through which the soul is said to pass at the moment of death. In many parts of Asia and Europe, it is felt that the soul departs through the chimney, smoke hole, or roof. To facilitate this passage in cases of prolonged illness, one or more boards are removed from the roof of the sick person's dwelling or the roof is even broken open.

Architecture can also be seen as completing the needs of the mind and body. It provides shelter from the elements, a place to cook and eat, a setting to bathe and sleep. By physically supporting the renewal of the spirit, architecture can become a means of healing. The ancient Egyptians saw this connection in the personality of Imhotep, whom they simultaneously called the first architect and physician. In our everyday experience, mind, body, and architecture are joined through six modalities of form and function—life-support systems, the five elements, measurement, proportion, gravity, and action.

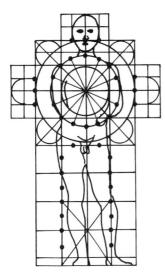

Human shape in church plan, after di Giorgio.

LIFE-SUPPORT SYSTEMS

Consciousness flows into matter through the body's life-support systems. The inward and outward flow of awareness finds physical expression in the mechanism of the lungs. Architecture extends the stream of inner intelligence that flows through the body into structural elements. Doors and windows become the lungs of a house.

Respiratory, circulatory, excretory, and other life-support systems are not confined by our outer layer of skin. Where does the air in our lungs begin and the air of the earth's atmosphere leave off? What is the boundary line that divides the fluids that course through our veins from the water that flows in the rivers of the world? The functioning of the body extends through our skin and our architectural "skin," to include the life of the whole planet. As the hero of the Jicarilla Apache, Killer of Enemies, said,

> The world is just as big as my body. . . . The seasons are only as great as my body. It is the same with the water. . . . Don't think I am in the east, south, west, or north. The earth is my body. I am over there. I am all over. Don't think I stay only under the earth or up in the sky, or only in the seasons, or on the other side of the waters. These are all my body. I am all over.

Breath creates the fundamental link between mind, body, and architecture. Without breathing, the whole mechanism of the body ceases to function. The seers of ancient India called the life force within our breath *prana*—the power of consciousness to manifest itself as the material universe. When prana assumes a subjective quality, they said, it becomes mind; taking on an objective quality, it becomes matter, making it the vital link between our thoughts and the environment. The concept of prana extends to include architecture and landscape design in the five-thousand-year-old building science of Vedic architecture, called *sthapatya-veda*, which recommends unrestricted cross ventilation, abundant green space, and fountains, lakes, and other water elements. In this way buildings and landscape become external lungs that continuously purify and refresh the prana in the air.

The Chinese system of architecture and environmental design called *feng shui* considers *ch'i*—the Taoist equivalent of prana—the most important component in designing human habitats. One expert explained that the only thing necessary to practice feng shui is the ability to recognize ch'i. This is because ch'i is said to be the animator of all things—breathing life into plants and animals, forming mountains by inflating the earth, and carrying water through channels in

Every man is the builder of a temple called the body.
Thoreau

I do with a building as I do with a man, watch the eye and the lips: when they are bright and eloquent, the form of the body is of little consequence.
John Ruskin

*A striking building stands
before us as an individual every
bit as soulful as we are.*
Thomas Moore

*The secret of the idea of a
blessing to be found in the
holy places lies in this
principle, that the holy place
is no longer a place; it has
become a living being.*
Hazrat Inayat Khan

the ground. It determines the health and vitality of mountains, trees, waterways, and people. All things affect each other by inhaling and exhaling ch'i. In the traditional Chinese disciplines of acupuncture and martial arts, knowledge of ch'i is essential. As with prana, ch'i is considered the link between spirit and matter, and these arts are intended to facilitate a smooth flow of ch'i between mind, body, and environment. Feng shui experts accomplish this by designing buildings, landscapes, and furniture to promote a balanced and unobstructed flow of ch'i. Accordingly, the best building site is considered to have the shape of a protective armchair, backed by a high hill on the north, with a lower hill on the east and west, and a body of water to the south. The house would be ideally placed halfway up the middle hill. This formation provides protection from northerly winds and opens to the ch'i-filled sunlight and refreshing southerly breezes blowing across the water. A plot of land or a building is best, they say, if it has a balanced shape, such as a square or rectangle. A seventeenth-century author described the experience of an environment with these qualities:

> There is a touch of magic light. . . . It can be understood intuitively, but not conveyed in words. The hills are fair, the waters are fine, the sun handsome, the breeze mild; and the sky has a new light; another world. Amid confusion, peace; amid peace, a festive air. Upon coming into its presence, one's eyes are opened; if one sits or lies, one's heart is joyful. Here *ch'i* gathers, and the essence collects. Light shines in the middle, and magic goes out to all sides.

The flow of information through the body is another vital factor linking our health and well-being to the environment. The nervous system coordinates and controls information within the body, influencing our consciousness and behavior. It is a communication network that allows cells to "talk" to one another in order to combat disease, that regulates the intake of oxygen, monitors the flow of fluids, and manages other bodily functions. Communication in any system occurs at its junction points. The ancient system of Indian medicine, Ayurveda, calls the vital intersections within the body *marma*s. Like the meridians mapped out by Chinese acupuncture, marmas are invisible to the eye but accessible through the sense of touch. Marmas can be stimulated to maintain balance in the body and enliven consciousness. Ayurvedic surgical texts warn against cutting across the marmas. This concept was translated directly into Vedic building form. It was felt that an organizing intelligence lived within every building; its body was embedded in the floor. Placing a pillar or a wall on any of the architectural marma points of this body was considered abusive to the intelligence dwelling within the building.

FIVE ELEMENTS

Since ancient times matter has been said to consist of five elements—earth, water, fire, air, and space. These are not the chemical elements described in the chart of atomic weights and numbers but are qualities of consciousness or patterns of intelligence that portray the characteristics of physical form. Earth is said to express the spiritual attributes of stability, support, and firmness; water, the features of fluidity, translucency, receptivity, surrender, nourishment, and sparkle; fire is warm, radiant, and clear; air is flexible, light, transparent, and soft; space exhibits the qualities of transcendence, openness, expansion, and potentiality.

Every architectural form and part of the body can be described as a combination of the five elements. A curved staircase, for instance, displays earth in the support of each tread, water in the fluid shape of its handrail, fire in its color and shades of light and shadow, air in its rise above gravity, and space in the gaps between the balusters and treads. The form and function of your hand expresses earth in its firmness, water in the folds of the skin, fire in its warmth, air in its dexterity, and space between the fingers.

The physical attributes of these elements are connected to the mind and body through the five senses. Sound is transmitted through the medium of space and is related to hearing; air is related to touch; fire to sight; water to taste; and earth to smell. Since our experience of architecture is received through the senses, the design of its form and function can be understood as a composition of the five elements. The sounds of a concert hall describe the quality of its space; the texture of its floor, walls, and ceiling convey its air, or atmosphere; its color and lighting sparkle with fire; the fluid curves of the balcony or seats describe the tastefulness of its design; and the wafting of perfume or other aromas impart its smell.

Numbers are sources of form and energy in the world. They are dynamic and active even among themselves . . . almost human in their capacity for mutual influence.
Theon of Smyrna

What is God?
He is length, width, height,
and depth.
St. Bernard
of Clairvaux

MEASUREMENT

Every physical object has a height, width, and depth. These measurements provide another means of connecting mind, body, and architecture. The mind constantly "sizes up" the surrounding conditions. We compare apples and oranges, high and low, friend and foe. Terms like *knee-high* and *arm's length* are derived from the sizes of the body's various parts. Architecture is constructed by joining materials with precise measurements: two-by-four lumber, "sixteen-penny" nails, quarter-inch screws.

The mind is linked to architecture by the size of the body and its various parts. The thought "I want to cook a meal," for example, is directly connected to a kitchen by the measurements of the body. Countertops are placed at a height that facilitates cutting or mixing; the height of the ceiling, dimensions of the cabinets and appliances, and floor area required to move about are all derived from human size. In India the width of a forefinger was the basic measuring unit; the foot determines the height, width, and depth of buildings in the United States and England. The cubit is an ancient unit of measure derived from the length between the end of the middle finger and the elbow. The *Mayamata* describes a precise system of measurement used by Vedic builders.

Consciousness is connected to architecture by the size and shape of the body. The shape of a chair, height of a shelf, and width of a doorway reflect the intimate links between the mind, body, and environment.

All habitations are defined by their dimensions. . . . The *manangula* is known to be a multiple of an atom, defined as that which can be perceived by the vision of those who have mastered their senses [yogis or sages]. Eight atoms are equal to a speck of dust and, in multiplying each time by eight, we go from a speck of dust to the tip of a hair, then to a nit, to a louse, and finally to a grain of barley. Eight barley grains make a digit (*angula*). . . . Twelve digits make a span (*vitasti*) twice which is a cubit (*hasta*) . . . twenty-five digits make a *prajapatya*, twenty-six a *dhanurmusti* and twenty-seven a *dhanurgraha*. For vehicles and seats the cubit is used, for buildings the *dhanurmusti* and for villages and so on the *dhanurgraha*. . . . The *matrangula* is equal to the middle phalanx of the middle finger of the officiating priest; it is to be used for measurements relating to sacrifices, etc.; that which has been mentioned is also called "digit taken from the body."

Mayamata

Scale is a concept of measurement that intimately connects mind, body, and architecture. We perceive scale in four basic ways. The first is in sensing the way that one object relates to the wholeness of an entire place. A staircase is smaller in scale than a house. Another way is to relate one part of a building to another part. The space within a closet is smaller in scale than the space within a bedroom. Scale is also perceived in terms of an object's usual size. In most homes a door is six feet eight inches tall. Encountering a door that is eight or ten feet tall causes a perceptual shift in our experience. The way we perceive an object or space in relation to the human body is the most important means of scaling our surroundings, however. Experiences of intimacy or expansiveness are created by unconsciously comparing the size of our bodies to the size of the walls, pillars, and other architectural elements around us. The body is the measure of all things.

PROPORTION

Proportional measurement allows the dimensions of mind, body, and architecture to encompass sacred wholeness. Throughout history the geometric proportions of the human body have been seen as expressions of divine intelligence, bringing coherent form to the material world. Luca Pacioli, the Renaissance mathematician and friend of Leonardo da Vinci, wrote in his *De divina proportione*:

> First we shall talk of the proportions of man, because from the human body derive all measures and their denominations and in it is to be found every ratio and proportion by which God reveals the innermost secrets of nature. . . . After having considered the right arrangement of the human body, the ancients proportioned all their work, particularly temples, in accordance with it. For in the human body they found two main figures without which it is impossible to achieve anything, namely the perfect circle . . . and the square.

The illustrations accompanying Pacioli's text were drawn by none other than Leonardo, who gave us the well-known drawing of a human figure placed within the outlines of a circle and square—the one seen on everything from vitamin bottles to automobile ads.

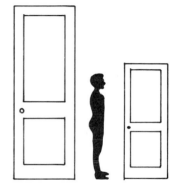

Our experience of scale reflects the tendency of the mind to categorize the objects around us according to their size (top). The size of architectural elements in relation to our bodies can create an intimate or monumental sense of scale (bottom).

The architects, artists, musicians, and theoreticians of Renaissance Italy believed that such illustrations expressed timeless truths that connected the mundane world to the sacred. These thinkers drew on the Pythagorean idea that a mathematical and harmonic structure informed the entire creation, including the human spirit. The architect Leon Battista Alberti maintained that the harmony perceived through the senses reflects the harmony of the soul. This implied that a building designed in accordance with archetypal harmonies provided the direct experience of the vital energies that uphold all matter and bind the universe together. Accordingly, prayer could not be effective in a church unless it related the microcosmic proportions of humans to the macrocosmic harmonies of God. Pacioli and other writers went so far as to say that sacred rites have little value if a church has not been built "with correct proportions."

The circle was considered the most perfect geometric shape and the clearest symbol of divinity. God was seen as a circle whose center is everywhere and circumference is nowhere. This geometric definition of God through the symbol of the circle reaches as far back as the Orphic poets of ancient Greece. Plato made it the central idea of a cosmological myth in his *Timaeus;* it was a key notion in the writings of Plotinus and the works of medieval theologians. Lame Deer says that the primary symbol of Native Americans is the circle—the hoop. He observes that the bodies of human beings and animals have no corners and that the circle stands for harmony among people who sit with one another around the campfire. In Lakota camps, the tepees are laid out in a circle, part of a larger hoop, the seven campfires of the Lakota, which form one nation. This nation is considered part of a circular universe made from the round earth, round sun, and round stars. The moon, the horizon, and the rainbow were created from circles within circles that have no beginning and no end.

Where the circle was seen as the image of transcendent power, the square was considered the symbol of the divine in material form. It represented the four directions of earthly existence—north, south, east, and west. Raising the square into three-dimensional form creates the fundamental building block of architecture—the cube. A circular dome placed on top of a cube symbolizes the unity of heaven meeting the diversity of earth. In the Islamic world, the ritual of circumambulating the cubic form of the Kaaba in Mecca offers a different inflection of combining the circle and square.

The Golden Proportion is regenerative, that is, it describes a set of laws which return to the One or to unity from multiplicity. Thus as a principle it expresses the idea of returning to the source or uniting again with divinity.
Richard Geldard

Vitruvian figure, after Leonardo. Renaissance artists, architects, and mathematicians thought that "every ratio and proportion by which God reveals the innermost secrets of nature" could be found in the human body.

The circle has long been seen as a clear symbol of the sacred. Many Renaissance churches were designed around the concept that "God is a circle whose center is everywhere and circumference is nowhere."

East

Most Plains tribes arranged their tepees in a circular pattern with an opening to the renewing power of the sunrise in the east (above). Pueblo kivas reflect this notion of wholeness (left).

While Leonardo's drawing of the Vitruvian figure depicts the overall proportions of the entire body within the circle and square, it also delineates the proportional relationships between the body's various parts. Leonardo pointed out that "every part is disposed to unite with the whole, that it may thereby escape from its incompleteness." These proportional relationships were called the golden proportion, because they not only united the diversity within the body but also appeared to bring coherence to numerous structures in nature. A sunflower, chambered-nautilus shell, and snowflake all have different shapes, but each finds harmony in the geometric relations of the golden proportion.

In this regard, musical harmonies captured the imaginations of Renaissance architects, artists, and philosophers. The ancient Greeks were credited with discovering that mathematical relationships in music were reflected in harmonious structures found in nature. Alberti wrote that

> the numbers by which the agreement of sounds affects our ears with delight, are the very same which please our eyes and our minds. . . .We shall therefore borrow all our rules for harmonic relations from the musicians to whom this kind of number is extremely well known, and from those particular things wherein Nature shows herself most excellent and complete.

Geometric harmonies inform architecture throughout the globe. A Vedic sutra declares, "The Universe is present in the Temple by means of proportion." The stone circles of the British Isles, the ziggurats of the Middle East, the Pyramids of Egypt, the temples of Greece and Rome, the pagodas of Japan, and the kivas of the Hopi are diverse expressions of cultures that have used the archetypal harmonies of the circle, square, and golden proportion. Gothic builders placed on their cathedrals the image of Christ holding a compass, a symbol of the Cosmic Architect. They felt that using sacred geometries allowed them to transcend individual egotism to become instruments of divine will. The crystalline shapes of Persian architecture echo this theme. In Japan, the size of the rectangular tatami mat is based on the amount of space one person needs for sleep. Rooms are proportioned by combinations of the basic tatami-mat unit; a

[A circular church] is enclosed by one circumference only, in which is to be found neither beginning nor end . . . and moreover every part being equally distant from the center, such a building demonstrates extremely well the unity, infinite essence, and justice of God.
Andrea Palladio

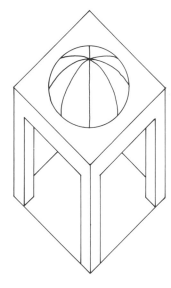

Dome on cube.

six-mat room, an eight-mat room, and so on. In 1942 the architect Le Corbusier published a system of proportion called the Modular that combined the aesthetic dimensions of the golden proportion and the functional measurements of the human body. He felt that this system could "maintain the human scale everywhere," and "lend itself to an infinity of combinations; it ensures unity with diversity . . . the miracle of numbers."

GRAVITY

Every object on the globe is pulled toward the earth's center by gravity. An unsupported roof beam or a person diving into a lake follow the same path as they surrender to gravity's call. This constant pull would be overwhelming if another equally important force did not counteract it. The attraction of the earth's mass is balanced by expansion away from its core. The mind/body/architecture relationship is a continuous interplay of contracting and expanding forces.

Gravity compresses the bricks of a pillar; simultaneously the bricks extend away from the earth's surface. Our muscles contract and expand with every move we make. A pillar imitates our human stance on the earth's surface, reflecting both our burdens and our hopes. A building's structural system is a mental concept, engineered to balance contractive and expansive forces. This condition is reflected in our skeletal and muscular system. The bones of the feet spread out to create a platform that upholds the rest of the body. The legs act as two pillars, extending away from the earth's gravitational pull. The pelvis serves as a crossbeam, which in turn supports the spinal column. The shoulder blades act as another beam, supporting the neck and head. The domelike structure of the skull recalls the span of a roof.

A deep understanding of expansion and contraction allows us to use stone, heavy timbers, and other building materials in ways that take on the qualities of the human spirit. The flying buttresses and soaring heights of Gothic cathedrals are high-wire acts of architectural virtuosity. Medieval builders cut their stones with such precision that no mortar was needed; the stones pressed one against the other with a delicate balance that let tons of mass hurdle vast interior spaces, echoing the aspirations of those who worshiped inside. Mind and body shaped matter into the rising architecture of the soul.

All the animate and inanimate beings that comprise the universe, which has the form of an unbroken circle, are permeated by Brahman, which is beyond these.
Skanda Purana

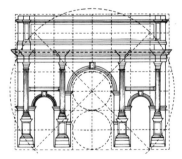

The Roman Arch of Septimius Severus is designed around the proportions of the circle and square. A grid of squares locates the gateways, pilasters, and crossbeams. Circles are used to define the arches and other details.

Through a deep understanding of structural forces, the builders of Chartres Cathedral created flying buttresses that defied gravity, echoing aspirations of the spirit (opposite).

There is health when the body is harmonized into unity, and beauty when the essence of unity controls the parts, and virtue in the soul when it is unified and brought into a single harmonious whole.
Plotinus

ACTION

Architecture is the residue of action. A chair, for example, serves as a direct expression of this principle, because its design corresponds to the body's size, shape, and function. The height of chair legs is derived from the average length of a person's leg, from the heel to the joint of the knee, allowing us to sit comfortably while our feet rest easily on the floor. The width and depth of the seat are proportioned to fit the part of the body that rests there. Often chair seats are molded to provide additional comfort, even if they are made of hard materials such as wood. Chair backs and arms are sometimes curved in proportions that elegantly receive the parts of the body that rest against them. A chair's comfort and usefulness are measures of how well it is contoured to fit the body and mind. Form, function, and sense of place are further refined by designing chairs for specific uses. A baby's high chair is a dining room in miniature, complete with table and seating at a sociable height for "conversation." Rocking chairs have a unique aura of graceful completeness, where the to and fro of living find balance. The colorful sling of a canvas beach chair celebrates the pleasures of summer, while the sturdy elegance of a Shaker chair efficiently serves the everyday functions of living. Thrones are designed to remind everyone within their presence that they are seats of power. A drafting stool's adjustable height and swivel accommodate the plethora of actions associated with its use. New ways of perceiving a chair can create unexpected uses—forts for children, not-so-sturdy ladders, haphazard coatracks, essential equipment for lion tamers, and secure perches for cats. In the midst of these functions, chairs bear witness to our history and store memories of living. A wooden arm is molded by the warm palm of the hand that rested there on countless summer evenings. The faded colors of an upholstered cushion record the passage of sunlight; the worn place recalls a favorite spot for sitting to read and dream. The curve of the legs or the flair of the back may reveal the style and flavor of the time a chair was made. The stainless-steel-edged, vinyl-seated dinette chairs of the 1950s seem perfect reflections of their times. The precious lines of a Louis XIV piece evoke the elegant air of royal life in seventeenth-century France.

Physics explains that every action yields an equal and opposite reaction. The Sanskrit word *karma* literally means action. It implies a direct correlation between the shape of mind/body activity and the

The elements of a child's bedroom respond to the actions of the body: a spiral staircase for stepping, a bed for sleeping, a bookcase for sitting against while reading.

forms in the surrounding environment. The body, for instance, takes on a stepping shape for climbing a staircase, which is reflected in the form of the treads that rise step by step one above the other. The Sanskrit word *yagya* indicates the way that psychology, physiology, and surroundings can be integrated in a unified whole. A yagya is commonly defined as a religious performance, but it can also be any action that furthers evolution. Taken beyond the narrow limits of a particular ceremony, yagya describes action that encourages transformations in consciousness and environment. Kneeling to receive the wine and wafer in the Latin Mass, lighting a candle in a chapel, placing flowers in a sacred river, and other actions performed with mindfulness can harmonize spirit and matter. "Yoga is skill in action," explains Krishna in the *Bhagavad Gita*. *Yoga* means union, the yoking of parts in wholeness and true skill in action—connecting mind, body, and architecture in sacred totality.

The mind is sheltered by the form and functioning of the body. How the natural environment completes the temple of human dwelling is discussed in the next chapter.

Seeing and Creating

1. Notice how the vital processes of your body—breathing, circulating fluids, maintaining body temperature, sensing the environment, and eliminating waste—are expressed in your home. Imagine your house as a living being that requires nourishment, cleansing, and affection.

2. Locate the qualities of the five elements—earth, water, fire, air, and space—in an architectural element or piece of furniture. How does the form of this object express earth's stability, water's receptivity, fire's light, air's softness, and space's expansiveness?

3. Become aware of the relationship between the size of your body and the size of the objects you use—how a doorknob or fork fits your hand. How could these objects be redesigned to create a better fit with your body? Notice the size of the different architecture you pass through during the day and how this affects your consciousness. Imagine what your home, office, and city would be like if they were twice their usual size or one half of it.

4. Look in a full-length mirror to become aware of your body's proportions—the relationship between height and width—in both standing and sitting positions. Notice how the objects in the room relate to your proportions. Is the relationship of height to width similar or different? Are the objects more squat or slender than you are? How could you refine or change the proportions of the walls, windows, and furnishings in the room to create a place that better corresponds to your consciousness?

5. Perceive the force of gravity that is pulling the ceiling, upper floors, and roof of your house to the center of the earth. See how the walls and pillars counteract that gravity, holding the house away from the earth. Lie on the floor or bed and feel gravity's pull into the earth. Stand up and feel how your skeletal and muscular systems counteract gravity.

6. Be mindful of how the architecture you encounter on a typical day responds to your movements. Notice how streets give access to buildings, how a revolving door turns as you enter, how stairs lead to an upper floor. How might you redesign your kitchen, office, or other work area to better support your actions, making them more like a ceremony that savors life rather than an unconscious routine?

Sunlight and Renewal

The great fire at the beginning of the dawn has sprung aloft, and issuing forth from the darkness has come with radiance. Agni, the bright-bodied, as soon as born fills all dwellings with shining light.

When born, you, O Agni, are the embryo of heaven and earth, beautiful, born about in the plants; variegated, infantine, you disperse the nocturnal gloom; you issue forth roaring loudly from the maternal sources.

. . . You have ever sustained, Agni, both heaven and earth, as a son supports his parents; come, youngest of the gods, to the presence of those desiring you; Son of strength, bring the gods here.

RIG VEDA

Surrounding mind and body is the natural environment. Climate, terrain, plants, and animals constitute the outermost layer of the mind/body/environment temple. Within the boundless cosmos, the earth provides a firm place to dwell and the ecological processes that sustain life. The global ecosystem and its relationship to the planetary system and galaxy are too complex for the human intellect to fully comprehend. In order to grasp the wholeness of the mind/body/environment structure in buildings, we need to locate an organizing power that shapes architecture's relationship to this temple of the soul. One such golden thread that runs through nature's countless processes is sunlight.

Sunlight is the powerhouse of the earth's ecosystem. Climatic changes, photosynthesis in plants, and the circadian rhythms of animal species are driven by the sun. Without the sun's light, the earth would be a lifeless rock. Louis Kahn perceived a poetic relationship between sunlight and the material objects that constitute the environment: "All material in nature, the mountains and the streams and the air and we, are made of Light which has been spent, and this crumpled mass, called material, casts a shadow, and the shadow belongs to Light." The sun's reflection as moonlight is also an elemental force in human existence, associated with women's bodily cycles, times of planting and harvesting, the rise and fall of tides, and the measurement of time.

A primal connection exists between sunlight and moonlight and the making of architecture. We dwell in the rhythms of solar and lunar radiance. Working, eating, playing, and sleeping tend to follow the rhythm of dawn, noon, twilight, and night. Floors, walls, and roofs support these activities and shelter them from the heat and cold brought about by the sun's seasonal glow. The constantly changing play of sunlight throughout the day and year transforms buildings from lumps of dead matter into vital structures filled with life; its radiance brightens our spirits and enlivens our bodies. Sunlight unifies mind, body, and environment in architecture in five ways: orientation, cycles of renewal, shadow play, relationship to source, and sacred fire.

Architecture is the masterly, correct and magnificent play of masses brought together in light.
Le Corbusier

ORIENTATION

On the twenty-first day of the fourth month, Hidetsugu invited three friends to a predawn tea ceremony. When the guests arrived in the wee hours of the morning, they found the tearoom shrouded in darkness; a bubbling kettle offered the only greeting. After sitting in the stillness for a time, they became impatient and wondered why their host kept them waiting. One of the guests noticed the appearance of a faint glow on the *shoji*, a paper-covered window. Sliding it aside, the little group beheld the perfect circle of a full moon centered in the frame. The silver beams spread across the room, illuminating a scroll in the alcove, which read:

*When I lift my eyes
To the quarter of the sky
Where the cuckoo cried,
There is nothing to be seen
But the early morning moon.*

In the undifferentiated darkness of the night, the dawning of sun- and moonlight gives a direction to time and space. The chaos and confusion of cloudy consciousness is clarified, our perceptions gain a specific point of reference, and we discover our dwelling place in the world. *Oriens*, the Latin root of the word *orientation*, means "rising," and in referring to the rising sun it recalls the daily rebirth of the solar fire's life-giving power. Honoring the genesis of light has been a primary function of architecture throughout the globe. The indigenous people of Japan, the Ainu, created homes with east-facing entrances that allowed the rays of the morning sun to symbolically rekindle the central fire pit; crossing the entrance at this moment was discouraged since it would break the vital contact between brother sun and sister hearth. The tepees of the Great Plains also looked to the east and were arranged in village circles that opened in that direction. Greek, Roman, Egyptian, and Indian temples receive the dawn through eastern doorways. Gothic cathedrals are often aligned so that solar rays pierce the stained-glass windows of the apse, symbolically igniting the life of the altar. In Guatemala, the dawning sun determined the layout of the entire temple complex at Uaxactún; three temples to the east of the central temple marked the sunrise points at the solstices and equinoxes.

O You! Who dwell in the House of the Dawn, in the House of the Evening Twilight, where the Dark Mist curtains the doorway, the path to which is the Rainbow.
Anasazi prayer

Northeast
Sunrise June 21

East
Sunrise September 21 and March 21

Southeast
Sunrise December 21

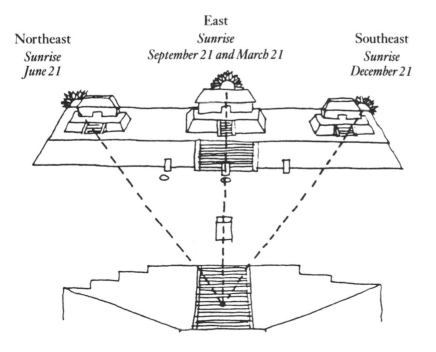

The temple complex at Uaxactún, Guatemala, was designed to honor seasonal cycles. Three temples to the east of the central temple mark the sunrises on the solstices and equinoxes.

117

Our relationship with sunlight continues to shape forms of dwelling as the globe revolves. Imagine yourself standing on the plain of a Nebraska wheat field. Day after day the sun appears to rise, ascend, and set, inscribing an east–west axis across the circular horizon. At noon the southern zenith of the solar path marks a southern direction and implies its opposite pole to the north. The intersection of these axes marks the four quarters of the world and outlines the primal architecture of four walls beneath a vaulting ceiling.

The more the Soul lives in the light of the Spirit, "turned toward" that which is above itself, the more creative it becomes.
Plotinus

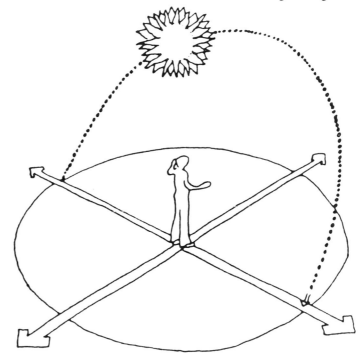

For thousands of years Indian architects and builders have used this relationship to the sun to create architecture. Using a staff, a cord, a circle on the earth, and sunlight, they follow a ritual procedure for drawing a network of arcs about a central pillar to delineate the ground plans of temples, houses, and cities. The ceremony is both a practical tool for building construction and a powerful metaphor for the way human consciousness perceives a sense of place in the universe. By mapping the unfolding of a specific site, the ceremony indicates a symbolic gateway to the source of all places.

With the dawning light of an auspicious day, the ritual of placemaking begins. Choosing the correct time is of the utmost importance; the specific arrangement of planets and stars at the moment of the structure's birth has implications for positive or negative influences on the health and prosperity of the future inhabitants. In the middle of the chosen site, the *sthapati* (architect) smoothes the earth. Serving as a practical step in preparing the building site for construction, this rite also encourages psychological stability in the minds of those about to build. In the midst of the leveled earth the *sutragrahin* (architect's assistant) sets up a gnomon fashioned of ivory, sandalwood, or other hardwood; two-dimensional flatness rises into three-dimensional space. Using the pillar as the central point and a length of cord as a radius, he etches the arc of a circle into the ground.

As the morning light stretches over the site, the gnomon throws a shadow across the circle. As the earth makes its daily revolution the long shadow gradually shortens, inching its way along the ground. By midmorning the shadow's tip converges on the edge of the circle. This point is marked. In the afternoon the shadow touches the opposite edge of the ring, and again the point is marked. Connecting these two points defines a perfect east–west axis.

Next, two more arcs are etched into the earth from the end points of the east–west axis. A line connecting these points delineates a north–south axis.

North–south and east–west axes are joined to establish a new central point. About this new center the sutragrahin draws a second circle.

About the new circle, two more carp shapes are drawn at right angles to each other.

Connecting the points where the two carp shapes overlap establishes a square that is used to create the footprint, or place, of the building and completes the place-making ritual.

This ancient ritual mimics the archetypal development of place and space, tracing the six directions that frame all sensory experience: front, back, left, right, up, and down. Based on this place-making ritual, Indian temples, homes, and cities were designed to harmonize with the rhythms of the sun and moon. Rooms in a building and the various districts of a city were oriented to the various qualities of solar energy experienced at different times of the day. The quiet light of dawn was perceived as having a different level of vibration than the brilliant radiance of noon, the eventide at dusk, or the night's silvery moonlight. Daily activity also expressed a range of

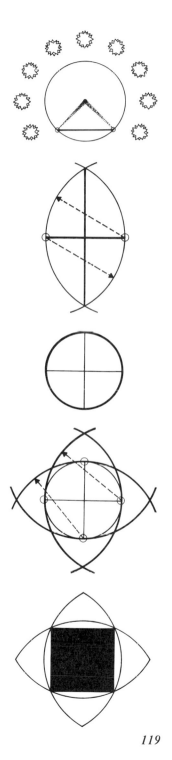

*You cannot understand the play
of relativity without being
immersed in the radiant
stillness of the Absolute.
Wherever there is butter, there
is buttermilk.*
Ramakrishna

frequencies—sleeping being less active than bathing, which in turn was less active than a social gathering. Vedic architecture, therefore, oriented the rooms of a house so that the activities taking place in different areas faced the quality of sunlight that best supported that activity—the dining room being oriented to the solar direction that was most conducive to digestion, the bedroom to rest, and so on. By dwelling in buildings and communities designed on this principle, daily life became a pilgrimage, a journey along the luminous paths of sun and moon.

The Renaissance architect Andrea Palladio described a similar notion in his *Four Books of Architecture:* "Merchants' houses ought to have places facing the north. . . .What contributes also to convenience is, that the rooms for summer be ample, spacious and turned to the north; and those for the winter be to the south and west. . . . But those which we would make use of in spring and autumn, must be turned to the east, and ought to look over greens and gardens. In this particular part, studies and libraries ought to be; because the morning is the most proper time of all to make use of them."

A contemporary version of a house as a diagram of the sun's path was designed in 1980 by Stanley Saitowitz. This unbuilt project was planned to orient its functions to appropriate solar directions. The entrance to Sundial House and the breakfast room were to face the east. The daytime activities of the living room were placed to the south, with evening dining to the west. To the north, where the sun doesn't travel, were the bedrooms; these had east-facing doorways so the morning's rays could, as Saitowitz said, "knock through each bedroom door to wake up the occupant." The curving vault of the roof traced the solar arc. On the east, three columns marked the sunrise of the summer solstice, equinox, and winter solstice. Four columns on the western wall represented the four seasons, and an arc of twelve columns stood for the months. Skylights in the roof worked together with the rafters to make a sundial.

CYCLES OF RENEWAL
*I died from mineral, and plant became;
Died from the plant and took a sentient frame;
Died from the beast, and donned a human dress;
When by my dying did I ever grow less. . . .*
Rumi

Attuning architecture to the sun and moon synchronizes the rhythms of our lives with the renewing cycles of nature. Solar light is born, develops, and dies each day, to be reborn the following dawn. Illumination expands and contracts in the seasonal rounds of winter, spring, summer, and autumn. Lunar rhythms of waxing and waning offer a vivid symbol of birth, death, and resurrection. Mythologies of every land deal with the theme of renewal. The Greeks called the killed and resurrected Dionysus "him of the double door." The European carnival games of Whitsuntide, Green George, John Barleycorn, Carrying Out Winter, Bringing In Summer, and Killing the Christmas Wren continued the tradition into the modern calendar. The Christian church echoes this theme in the Fall and Redemption, Crucifixion and Resurrection, and the "second birth" of baptism.

An old Shinto tale from Japan offers a delightful slant on this motif. It describes the reemergence of the sun goddess Amaterasu from a heavenly rock dwelling during a crucial time in the world's genesis. It seems that the storm god Susanowo, the goddess's brother, had been wreaking havoc throughout the realm. Amaterasu tried her best to placate him and expanded her compassion to the fullest, but he persisted in bringing chaos to society and demolishing the rice crops. Finally he smashed a hole in the roof of Amaterasu's weaving hall and let a piebald horse fall through the opening, which so startled the ladies who were weaving clothes for the deities that they died of fear.

The event terrified Amaterasu, and she fled to the safety of a heavenly cave. The entire universe was plunged into darkness, and anarchy reigned. Without the sun, life would cease to exist before it had really begun. Evil forces caused disarray throughout creation; the signs of catastrophe were everywhere.

In order to turn the tide, the eight million gods held a divine assembly in the bed of the tranquil river of heaven. A deity named Thought-Includer devised a plan that employed a mirror, a sword, and offerings of cloth. Jewels were used to adorn a great tree, bonfires were ignited, sutras were chanted, roosters were gathered to keep up an incessant crowing. The mirror was bound to the tree's branches. A young goddess named Uzume performed a wild dance that caused the eight million divinities to laugh so loudly that the heavens shook.

From her hiding place in the cave the sun goddess heard the commotion and wondered what was happening. She peered out and spoke to the throng: "I thought that my retirement would fill the plain of

Isn't it true that a pleasant house makes winter more poetic, and doesn't winter add to the poetry of a house?
Thomas De Quincey

121

heaven and the central land of reed with darkness. Why are Uzume and the eight million gods laughing?" Uzume replied, "We rejoice because there is a deity more glorious than you." At this moment two of the gods moved the mirror into a position where Amaterasu could see her own radiant reflection. The more she gazed at her luminous form, the more the sun goddess's amazement increased, gradually drawing her from the cave. A mighty god took Amaterasu's hand and pulled her all the way out, while another stretched a rope called a *shimenawa* behind her, across the cave's entrance, and said, "Thou must not return beyond this point!" Whereupon the creation was again filled with light. Every night the sun retreats for a time, in refreshing sleep, but a shimenawa prevents her from vanishing forever. The shimenawa is still used today at the gateways of Japanese shrines. It denotes the renovation of the world at the threshold of return.

In this matter of self and other, everything is Buddha without exception.
Buddhist Sutra

Shimenawa *are hung above the entrances to Japanese shrines at the New Year festival, symbolizing the time and place of renewal.*

Marking the limits of sunlight with architectural boundaries can be seen in many parts of the globe. The megaliths of Stonehenge are thought to have acted as a huge cosmological "clock" for sighting and predicting solstices, equinoxes, and eclipses of both sun and moon, the most notable event being the sunrise of the summer solstice. At

Ballochroy, a desolate stretch of moorland on the southwest coast of Scotland, three large stone slabs were placed in a line pointing toward a massive stone box one hundred feet to the west. If one stands by these stones at sunset on the winter solstice, the sun appears to descend into the box, which is thought to be the remains of a burial monument. A collective burial place was constructed in about 3300 B.C. at New Grange in eastern Ireland. The structure was decorated with magnificent carvings of spirals and other abstract designs, while its centerpiece seems to be a slot over the gateway to the tomb. Shortly after dawn at midwinter, a ray of light penetrates this slot and reaches to the back of the seventy-foot-long burial chamber, lighting up the stone basin placed there to receive the cremated remains of the dead.

On the American Great Plains, medicine wheels were constructed to coordinate human life with solar, lunar, and stellar cycles. About fifty of the ancient wheels have been discovered along the eastern foothills of the Rocky Mountains. Some are believed to have been in use since around 2500 B.C.—making them contemporary with the Egyptian Pyramids and the early stages of Stonehenge. Since the stone wheels were built by nomadic tribes, they have nothing to do with the practical economics of planting and harvesting. They embody what Joseph Campbell has called "mystical economics," the activities that attune human life to universal rhythms in order to assure well-being and prosperity. Observations taken at the Big Horn Medicine Wheel, near Sheridan, Wyoming, imply its use for this purpose. Placed at 9,640 feet above sea level, with an unobstructed view of the horizon, the wheel is designed to mark the sunrise and sunset on the summer solstice. The position of Aldebaran, the brightest star in Taurus's constellation, in its brief, first appearance in the dawn sky is also designated. After one "moon," or twenty-eight days, Rigel, Orion's most brilliant star, is marked by another position on the medicine wheel. Another moon of twenty-eight days is indicated by an alignment with Sirius, the sky's most luminous star. Before the next twenty-eight-day cycle has elapsed, the winter snows arrive, covering the wheel until June of the following year.

Twenty-eight lines of stones fan out from the hub of the medicine wheel to its rim. Interestingly enough, the sun-dance lodges of the northern Plains tribes are usually constructed of twenty-eight poles encircling a central axial pillar, which supports twenty-eight

Objects around are perceived, and from them the individual proceeds to contemplation of his own inner being . . . then inactive meditation is quitted for activity; by the close of the day, man has erected a building from his own inner sun.
Hegel

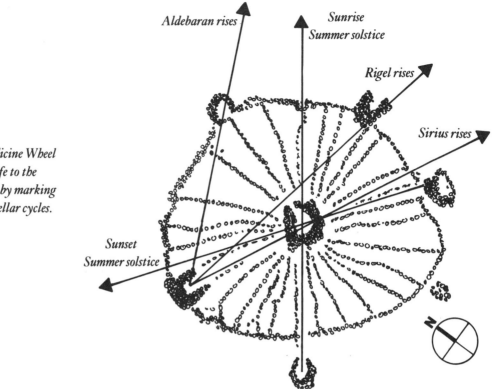

Aldebaran rises

Sunrise
Summer solstice

Rigel rises

Sirius rises

*The Big Horn Medicine Wheel
links human life to the
patterns of nature by marking
solar and other stellar cycles.*

Sunset
Summer solstice

N

roof beams. Even though there is no evidence that the nineteenth-century Lakota who built these lodges knew the purposes of the great medicine wheels, they intuitively continued their ancestral traditions by beginning their sun dances on the summer solstice.

A gesture toward "mystical economics" was implied by Palladio's Villa Barbaro of 1557. The villa was designed to integrate the life of a sophisticated, urbane client with the workaday functions of a rural farm near Venice. The Barbaro family lived in a templelike central pavilion of the complex that linked two wings of outbuildings used for agricultural functions. At the ends of the wings are two pavilions that sport astronomical instruments for measuring solar cycles. One device measures the hours of the day, the other calculates the signs of the zodiac. Although accurate calendars had been developed long before the construction of the villa, making the devices unnecessary, sunlight's daily and seasonal cycles were honored and integrated with the architecture. The instruments helped to create a setting where Daniele Barbaro could mingle his scholarly interests with practical farming activities to fulfill his concept of "holy agriculture."

*The rhythms of worship are
displayed by a sundial at
Chartres Cathedral.*

The elaborate observatories built by the Maharaja Jai Singh in Jaipur and Delhi during the eighteenth century display the sculptural possibilities of wedding the light of the sun, moon, and stars to architectural form. Ninety-foot-tall sundials, beautifully carved bowls for sighting the planets, and other magnificent shapes mirror the geometry of the sun, moon, planets, and stars. These instruments allowed those who used them to perceive the patterns of the heavenly bodies at specific times and to make astrological calculations. By providing glimpses of the past, present, and future, they revealed the sequential unfolding of an individual's destiny and his personal relationship to cosmic forces. The enormous size of the astronomical devices required a person to position himself at various locations within the structures to take observations, making his body an integral part of the instruments. Perceiving the rhythmic movements of planets and

It is not what we do,
it is how much love we put out
in the doing.
Mother Teresa

Agricultural rhythms are
marked by a zodiac dial at
the Villa Barbaro.

stars in this setting transcended a purely mental exercise to become a deeply felt physical experience—aligning individual consciousness with cosmic design.

Using light's cycles of renewal to shape architectural form extends to our own time. A 1991 Florida office building by Arata Isozaki & Associates for Team Disney is built around an immense sundial. Joining the two wings of the structure is a cone-shaped rotunda that opens to the sky. A boomlike gnomon projects over the sky door, casting a shadow on the courtyard's walls. Bands of colored tile mark the shadow lines that occur on the solstices and equinoxes. The floor of the sundial court is made of washed river rock, recalling the "dry streams" found in Japanese temple gardens. The court can only be traversed on a circular walk of granite stepping-stones that are etched with quotes about time, an intimate partner of solar and lunar cycles.

The beautiful sculptural shapes of Vedic observatories mirror the geometry of the heavens. A misra yantra, or mixed instrument, in New Delhi can indicate the solar time at Greenwich, Zurich, and other locations on the globe.

*The domed ceiling of the
Council Chamber at the
Mississauga Civic Centre in
Canada depicts the Mississauga
Indian legend of the Great
Bear and the Seven Hunters as
it appears in the constellations
of an evening
spring sky over the city.*

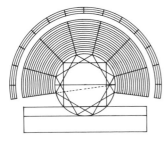

*The Roman architect
Vitruvius wrote in the first
century B.C. that the plans for
these structures were drawn
"as astrologers do in a figure of
the twelve signs of the zodiac,
when they are making
computations from the musical
harmony of the stars."*

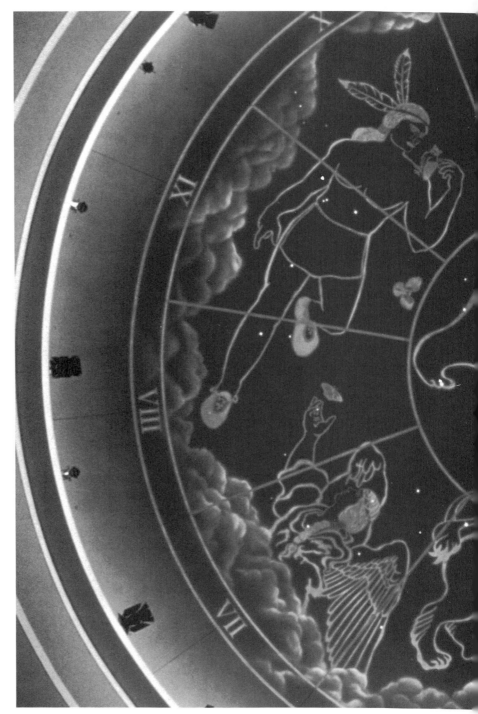

Our contemporary mind-set assumes that time moves in a line from past to future. In solar and lunar time, however, events repeat themselves; the sun rises daily, the moon continues to wax and wane. The sundial, therefore, becomes the perfect symbol for Disney, since its theme parks constantly play on our assumptions about time. They offer the promise of freely moving to any era in the past, present, or future—from Frontierland to Tomorrowland, from adulthood back to childhood. Amid the computers, budget reviews, and other business functions of Team Disney's adjacent offices, the sundial court offers a core of silence where one can stand on a bed of river stones, experience the sun's shadow sliding along the courtyard walls, and find the sacred power connecting architecture, earth, and sky.

Art is a
harmony parallel to nature.
Cézanne

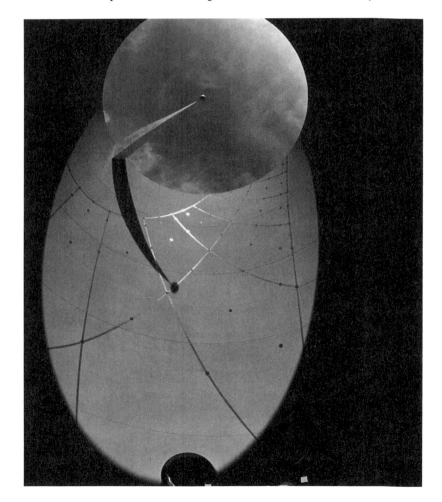

A gnomon projects over the sky door of the Sundial Court of the Team Disney Building in Orlando, Florida, casting a shadow that marks the sun's daily and seasonal cycles.

SHADOW PLAY

The pyramid, echoing silence, gives the sun its shadow.

Louis Kahn

Without shadow, light cannot be perceived. Pure light is as blinding as pitch darkness. Distinctions between the luminous and the shadowy reveal the contours of spoons, chairs, and cathedrals. Look around you and notice the innumerable shadings and subtle nuances of shadow's play. A curving vase, for example, reflects a smooth transition from brightness to shade. The entire environment is an ensemble of glowing surfaces, displaying radiant possibilities.

The Greek philosopher Heraclitus believed that all things tend to move upward from the moist and dark to the dry light of fire. Sacred architecture urges us to travel through this spectrum of light and shadow. Standing beneath the dome of San Carlo alle Quattro Fontane in Rome, for instance, we are shrouded in murky shadows; our sight is drawn upward to the lantern at the dome's apex, where a dazzling glow calls our spirits to rise heavenward.

The gardens of the Villa Lante outside Rome are shaped by primal notions of light and dark. The central axis of the garden passes through a dense forest to an open plain. Deep within the forest, a grotto encompasses an earthy domain of irregular rock outcroppings, wetness, thick vegetation, and darkness. As we move away from the grotto and down the garden path, the environment becomes more open and ordered until it reaches its ultimate transformation in a highly geometric courtyard. This tangible design reflects the Renaissance view that wild nature is chaotically dark and should be controlled by the light of reason.

Polarities of light and dark take a different architectural inflection at the Vietnam Veterans Memorial in Washington, D.C. Like an open wound, the polished black granite wall of the monument slices into a grassy knoll. Its core is reached by descending a path of rough granite pavers. The names of Americans slain in the war are cut into the dark rock face; shifting reflections of those walking along the polished wall mingle with the chiseled characters. Visitors search the expanse of stone, looking for the name of someone they knew; finding a familiar name, their faces fill with emotion as souls touch in a momentary reunion. Two paths rise out of the memorial; one points to the towering obelisk of the Washington Monument, the other leads to

It is the nature of any organic building to grow from its site, come out of the ground into the light.
Frank Lloyd Wright

131

The sun never knew how great it was until it struck the side of a building.
Louis Kahn

In houses that look toward the south, the sun penetrates the portico in winter, while in summer the path of the sun is right over our heads and above the roof so there is shade.
Socrates

the massive temple of the Lincoln Memorial. Made of gleaming white marble, both stand in sharp contrast to the black granite of the Veterans Memorial. The Washington Monument bolts skyward, an axial pillar of hope that captures the rising spirit of a new nation. The Lincoln Memorial embraces peace and reconciliation within the pillars that mark its perimeter. Together the three monuments embody a spectrum of emotion—from the searing pain of psychic wounds to the healing embrace of unity.

Another interpretation of light and dark is expressed in the murky interiors of traditional Japanese architecture. Rather than seeing beauty and goodness in brilliant illumination, the Japanese thought these qualities lived in the obscurity of shadows. Temples, palaces, and common homes were dominated by massive roofs. Architects built the enclosing structure of the various rooms in the deep, ample shadows produced by the eaves. Even in the most intense sunlight, the walls, doors, and pillars sheltered by the roof's edge disappeared in gaping darkness. Light was held out to the sides by the umbrellalike roof and penetrated the interiors horizontally through layers of shoji screens. Dwelling in the resulting darkness, the Japanese came to find beauty in gradations of shadows—heavy shadows overlapping lighter ones. In the simple, bare rooms, the nuances of faintly glowing surfaces became the sole decoration. The edges that separated one object from another dissolved to reveal the transcendent reality of things. Shadow's invisible details conveyed a silent power that no starkly lit painting or ornament could match.

RELATIONSHIP TO SOURCE

Plato's famous allegory of the cave describes a group of people facing the depths of a rocky chamber. Light pours through the opening behind them, casting shadows of outside objects on the cave's inner wall. Those dwelling inside are convinced that the shadows form the only reality of existence. A few leave the chamber and discover the cause of the interior shadows. When they return to the cave, however, they find it impossible to convince those who remained inside that another reality exists. The chains of rigid thinking bind them to the shadowy realm.

This allegory uses the physical structure of a cave to convey Plato's notion of our relationship to the source of life. Architecture is also a tangible expression of the ways we see our relationship to life's source. Palladio's Villa Capra of 1550, for example, diagrams the idea that human consciousness is the center of all things, "the kingdom of heaven is within." A rotunda delineates the middle of the four-square plan; the porticoes outline a symbolic compass, pointing to the cardinal directions. Inhabitants can occupy the midpoint of this arrangement, surveying the four quarters of space. Frank Lloyd Wright's Willits House defines a cosmos in which firelight occupies the core. The hearth's massive chimney fixes a central axis about which family life and the world revolve. In this plan, one can merely observe the sacred fire; human existence has a center that is outside itself. The Villa Savoye by Le Corbusier portrays a third paradigm—life as a field of energy that gives rise to events that fluctuate in time and space. The house is set on an expanse of lawn. It is offered up to sunlight on supporting columns that are arranged in an orthogonal grid that implies an undifferentiated extension of order in all directions. Within this grid, human activity moves freely through the sunlight that floods the interior. Events rise and fall within an even glow of light. One has access to the power of this field at any point in space and time. In this paradigm every place becomes sacred.

SACRED FIRE

Light's sacredness also resides in its power to generate heat. Prometheus stole the fire reserved for the gods and spread its potent magic to the world. The Vedic god Agni was born in the fire produced by rubbing celestial and terrestrial worlds together like two sticks. He thus became the son of heaven and earth and the brother of Indra, king of the gods. Where Indra gave air to humankind, Agni offered the vital spark, in heaven as the sun, in the atmosphere as lightning, and on earth as the sacrificial fire and nourishing hearth.

In the presence of solar fire, life germinates and expands. Existence is sustained, however, between a narrow range of temperatures. Architecture tempers the sun's heat by creating livable microclimates—warm and dry in the winter, cool in the summer. Walls, roofs, windows, awnings, and other devices enable mind, body, and environment to coexist in thermal comfort.

Many animal species, including ourselves, follow or retreat from the sun in seasonal migrations. Going to Florida in the winter and Cape Cod in the summer is a tradition that allows many New Yorkers to maintain thermal harmony with their environment. In the Ameri-

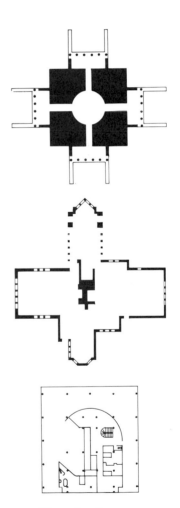

Floor plan diagrams:
Villa Capra, Willits House,
Villa Savoye.

An entire community took refuge from the intense heat at Mesa Verde. These Anasazi cliff dwellings are positioned below a massive rock ledge that provides shade from the high summer sun but allows the low rays of winter to warm the village.

can Southwest the Anasazi sited their cliff dwellings so that they would be shaded by overhanging cliff ledges in the summer and open to full sunlight throughout the winter. In our own homes we may be warmed by a sunny window in December and cooled by a covered, breezy porch in July. Activities in farming communities across the globe fluctuate with the cyclical rise and fall of solar radiance; planting takes place in the spring, harvest in the fall.

Bringing a bit of the sun's fire inside to the hearth has, throughout human history, provided a gathering point for family and community life. Cooking food and staying warm are aided by fire's magical properties—the glowing embers providing a tangible experience of the energies that transcend matter. Some scholars feel that the first structures were built to protect the sacred fire from wind and rain. The primordial house of many cultures—like the tepee—was essentially a fire pit sheltered by walls and a roof with a smoke hole at its apex. Hearths now take the shape of fireplaces, woodstoves, or kitchens.

The word *curfew* has its origins in the French *couvre-feu*, "cover the fire," reflecting the need to keep the hearth's fire burning continuously by covering it with ashes every night (some of the embers would then be glowing the following morning). Only during the death or birth of a household member was the fire ritually extinguished and rekindled. This tradition is continued by the Catholic Church during Easter, the celebration of Christ's death and resurrection. The night before Easter, all the lights in a church are put out before a new fire is ignited. From this blaze the Paschal, or Easter, candle is lit and spread to other candles throughout the church. The eternal flame that fires the Olympic torch, important grave sites, and other sacred places is an extension of the ever-glowing hearth at the center of the home.

In some countries an ember from the family hearth is brought to the new houses of married children. Ancient Greek mothers carried the *hestia* to their daughters' homes to ensure the continuation of family worship. Part of a traditional Indian wedding involves lighting a sacred fire that is taken to the couple's new house and used to kindle the family hearth. There it is employed for all domestic ceremonies throughout the couple's life, including the cremation of their bodies at death. Today we bring love and attention to new homes with housewarming parties. Because so many activities center around the hearth, fire serves as the home's animating spirit, becoming an outer reflection of the glowing consciousness that invigorates family life.

Whether people are fully conscious of this or not, they actually derive countenance and sustenance from the "atmosphere" of the things they live in or with.
Frank Lloyd Wright

This massive stone fireplace designed by Frank Lloyd Wright reflects the primal nature of sacred fire and establishes its importance at the center of the home.

Heat as a means of purification finds expression in the sweat lodge (*inipi*) of the Lakota. All ceremonies begin with time spent in this holy enclosure. A framework of twelve white willow wands corresponding to the twelve months of the year covered with tarps, blankets, or quilts form the sacred space. A small ridge of earth with a little *unci* (grandmother) mound at the end leads ten steps to the west of the hut.

Beyond the mound a fire called *owihankeshni* (the fire without end) for heating stones is ignited. It represents the flame that is handed down through time. Four sticks are laid in an east–west direction; four running north–south are placed on top of these. A cone of logs is built over the cross of sticks. It recalls the tepee, the primal dwelling within the six directions of space—north, south, east, west, above, and below.

According to Lame Deer, the sweat lodge's entrance faces the setting sun to the west. Two upright sticks and a crossbar are placed in front of the entrance, forming an altar for the sacred pipe. A bucket of clean, fresh water from a running stream is stationed nearby. The lodge is entered in a counterclockwise direction, with the leader seated near the entrance, one helper on the right, and another on the left; a third helper sits outside. This person brings in the heated rocks, which represent ancestors who have returned to earth. It is forbidden to come between him and the lodge by crossing his path. Traditionally a forked stick is used to carry the stones, but a pitchfork or similar implement is sometimes used. A prayer of thanks is spoken when the first rocks are handed through the opening. One of these is put in the center, representing grandmother earth. A cross of four stones pointing north, south, east, and west is then created. A sixth stone is put over the first one in the center, symbolizing grandfather spirit and the sky. Additional rocks are heaped on top of the initial group of six, up to fifty for special ceremonies.

Prayers are offered to the sacred stones: "They have no mouth, no eyes, no arms, nor legs, but they exhale the breath of life." The hut is then sealed off so no light can enter. Water is sprinkled on the red-hot rocks with a bit of sage, sweetgrass, or a ladle; heavenly rain touches the scorched earth. Clouds of intense steam fill the air, everyone's lungs draw in fire. If the heat is overwhelming, someone says, "*Mitakuye oyasin*" (all my relatives), and cool air is admitted through the entry. Icy water hisses on the scalding stones. The participants sing "*Tunka-shila, hi-yay, hi-yay,*" shaking the sweat lodge. Heat fills every pore with healing power. Elemental forces permeate body and mind.

In hot climates, wholeness is brought to mind, body, and environment by balancing the heat of sacred fire with cooling influences. If you have ever visited a place where the temperature ranges from hot to hotter, you know the refreshing experience of taking a dip in a

The supreme quality of beauty being a light from some other world [is] the idea . . . that matter is but a shadow, the reality of which is but the symbol.
James Joyce

river, finding relief in the shade of a spreading tree, catching an er-
rant breeze, or finding sanctuary within a thick-walled building.
Sacred coolness is created by employing four devices: water, shade,
flowing air, and massive stone or brick construction.

Water's sanctity is expressed in the holy rivers of the world. The
Nile, Ganges, and other great waterways serve as vital arteries of existence for millions of people and attest to the life-giving power of
coolness. At Benares, Calcutta, Hardwar, and numerous other cities
along the Ganges, for instance, stone steps (ghats) plunge down the
banks, offering pilgrims ready access to the holy wetness. Day after
day, year after year, a steady stream of worshipers flows into the renewing waters.

River water is caught in wells, tanks, fountains, and reflecting
pools, providing sacred cooling spots near temples and village centers. As early as 2000 B.C., temple tanks were built at Mohenjo-daro
to be used for purifying ablutions. Modern-day equivalents can be
found within temple precincts and beside roadways, where steps on
all four sides of the rectangular structures provide paths to the water.
One such tank at Adjalaj in northern India is itself a temple. Surrounded by desert, a series of columned terraces descends six stories
into the earth to reach the rising and falling waters of the well. Ritual
bathing takes place on each deepening stratum of the temple. Every
step downward offers a darker and cooler microclimate that culmi-
nates with a plunge into the holy waters. A bit of the well/temple is
carried home in water jugs, where it blesses the mundane functions of
living. The notion of water as a shrine is taken to the extreme at
Amritsar, where the Golden Temple stands in the middle of a
vast lake.

The classic image of the sage sitting beneath the branches of an
immense bodhi tree speaks of the sacred power of shade. Aryan
tribes built their communities around huge shade trees, which served
as axial pillars. Under the leafy canopies of these holy trees, students
learned sacred wisdom, the council of elders met, and religious festivals were held. Cooling breezes could move easily through these
outdoor rooms, bringing added comfort. The gazebos found at the
center of town squares throughout the Midwest echo the notion of
using a shade-giving structure, open to the air, as a community center. The colonnaded porches of Greek temples also mimicked the
shade and breezy atmosphere of trees. Acting like a little forest, the

The site for baths must be as warm as possible and turned away from the north. . . . They should look toward the winter sunset because when the setting sun faces us with all its splendor, it radiates heat, rendering this aspect warmer in the late afternoon.
Vitruvius

137

In hot climates, sacred places are created by providing shade. The natural cooling of a tree's leafy canopy (below) is imitated by a town-square gazebo (right) and a covered porch (lower right).

In Cairo, a room with fabric walls that can sway with the breeze offers a shadowy haven of coolness (left). The lacy structure of a garden pavilion in Cairo provides shade while remaining open to the slightest breeze (lower left).

columns and roof created shelter from the sun while remaining open to cooling air currents. In the arid deserts of northern Africa and the Middle East, a natural air-conditioning system was developed; towers reached aloft to catch the faintest breezes and funnel them into the depths of the building, where they passed over shaded pools of water.

Massive construction, refreshing breezes, and water are used in this Shiva temple to create sacred coolness.

Even greater relief from the heat is found in caves, the classic retreat of hermits, monks, and yogis. Besides lending an air of eternity, the massive amounts of stone and earth of these retreats temper the intense solar radiation, providing mild environments in the hottest climates. Countless religious structures were cut into the hillsides of Ethiopia, Anatolia, southern Italy, and the rest of the Mediterranean basin. Early Christian worship took place in the subterranean coolness and secrecy of the catacombs outside Rome. The Egyptian temples at Abu Simbel and the rock-cut Byzantine churches of central Asia Minor were monumental accomplishments. Some of the earliest Indian temples, such as those at Ellora and Mahabalipuram, were sculpted out of mountains; this technique influenced Indian religious architecture for more than a thousand years. A group of Buddhist monasteries was dug into the rock cliffs at Ajanta, in the Waghora River gorge. The pilgrims who arrived there from thousands of miles away found elaborately carved temples; moving toward the heart of these sanctuaries offered deepening layers of dark coolness.

The idea of using massive structures to make cooling environments was transferred to the mountainous stone temples of southern India. At Kancheepuram and Madurai, tall, pyramidal structures, called *vimana*s, shelter the shrines from the torrid sun. Refreshing breezes and water are also brought into play. The tall gateways catch the mildest wind and set up high-pressure zones that push turbulent air through the constricted passageway below, similar to the gusty conditions created by skyscrapers. Ablutions take place beside the temple in a water-filled tank. As worshipers enter the silence and coolness created by the temple's massive stone construction, a priest touches their foreheads with a spot of sandalpaste, adding to the cooling effect. In the American Southwest, the thick adobe walls used in pueblos, churches, and other buildings employ the same principle of mass to temper the intense heat. Massive brick construction also shapes cavernous Middle Eastern bazaars, creating bastions of shadowy coolness in the bustling centers of community life.

By orienting architecture to solar and lunar rhythms, mind and body are linked to nature's cycles of renewal. Human existence finds balance within the processes of nature. Part One delineated the facets of the temple of mind, body, and environment. In Part Two we will explore ways of applying this knowledge to your home, community, and world.

There is one Tirtha [sacred place] where one should always bathe and this is the Tirtha of the mind. It is deep, clear, and pure; its water is truth and metaphysical knowledge. Those who take this bath see the Principles, the true nature of things.
Mahabharata

The house, after all, is only a shell and the real interest must come from those who live in it. If this is done carefully and with earnestness it will give the inmates a sense of satisfaction and rest and will have the same power over the mind as music or poetry or any healthy activity in any kind of human experience.
Bernard Maybeck

141

Seeing and Creating

1. Observe the position of the sunrise and sunset at different times of the year in relationship to your house. Note these positions on March 21 and September 22 to locate a position close to due east and west. Note them on June 21 to the northeast and northwest and on December 21 to the southeast and southwest. Think of how you might use design elements such as sun symbols or even arrangements of furniture to connect your living environment to season cycles.

2. Imagine how the rooms of your house could be used in a way that allowed you to migrate with the sun during your daily routine. What activities would you put in the east, in the south, in the west, and in the north? How would you redesign your garden, or terrace, to attune it to the path of the sun and moon?

3. Bring your attention to the play of light and shadow in the room where you are sitting. Notice the smooth gradations of light on curving surfaces and the sharper transitions on angled objects. What qualities of consciousness do you associate with the different qualities of light and shadow? Adjust your vision to see the room purely as a play of the different qualities of light.

4. What attitude about humankind's relationship to the source of life does the floor plan of your home express? Is it consciousness-centered, with a core of open space that you can occupy; object-centered, with a fireplace or other element as a focal point; or an open field, with spots for random events to occur? What alternate layout would you choose to best express what you see as your relationship to the source of life?

5. How is sacred fire incorporated into your home? Notice the ways you savor heat in winter and coolness in summer. How might this experience of thermal delight be celebrated? Is there a fireplace that is given a prominent position? Could the cooking area be enhanced in some way to honor the nourishing qualities of fire in the stove? In summer, is there a way to incorporate the cooling influences of a covered porch or a shady spot in the garden into your daily routine?

PART TWO

Dwelling in the Sacred

SEVEN

Making a Sacred Place

Sacred space is a space that is transparent to transcendence, and everything within such a space furnishes a base for meditation. . . . When you enter through the door, everything within that space is symbolic, the whole world is mythologized.

To live in a sacred space is to live in a symbolic environment where spiritual life is possible, where everything around you speaks of the exaltation of the spirit.

This is a place where you can simply experience and bring forth what you are and what you might be. This is the place of creative incubation. At first you might find that nothing happens there. But if you have a sacred place and use it, something eventually will happen.

Your sacred space is where you find yourself again and again.

JOSEPH CAMPBELL

Our discussion so far has focused on how the temple of mind, body, and nature creates architecture that nourishes wholeness in life. These environments seem few and far between, however. Although most of us have visited shrines, churches, and other settings where sacredness is a palpable reality, these places usually remain outside the stream of day-to-day existence. If access to sacred sites is limited to a few rare and distant locations, the totality of our consciousness is restricted to those moments when the "profane" world can be left behind to enter a holy precinct. Since the sacred is the most intimate part of ourselves, we ought to be able to find it close at hand, in the immediate circumstances of daily existence. Spiritual architecture is not solely the province of religious structures dedicated to particular rituals and occasions. It can be created wherever the physical surroundings are shaped to give our lives depth and meaning. Every place—the concert hall, classroom, factory, and marketplace—can be sacred if the murmuring of the soul is allowed to shape the walls.

Tirtha is the name of a place of pilgrimage on the bank of a river, the seashore, or lake. The meaning of the word is a ford, or passage. [The current of water] which is the river of life can be forded in inner realization and the pilgrim can cross over to the other shore. The place of pilgrimage is the end of the journey to the Center; but it is not the goal itself and only a means for crossing over to the Center.
Stella Kramrisch

God's joy moves from unmarked box to unmarked box,
from cell to cell.
As rainwater down to the flowerbed.
As roses up from the ground.
Now it looks like a plate of rice and fish,
now a cliff covered with vines,
now a horse being saddled.
It hides within these,
till one day it cracks them open.

Rumi

In order to gain deeper, more intimate experiences of sacred places, we can try our hand at making them. Creating sacred places provides an opportunity to forge more personal connections to our immediate surroundings. It can be a self-empowering act that extends the full range of our consciousness into the physical world, a concrete means of restoring wholeness to the disparate threads of our lives.

Sacred places can be created on many scales. A shelf in the corner of a room can become a tiny altar, a window onto the deep spaces of the soul. The pages of a diary contain a universe of personal meaning. A room set aside for meditation and study provides access to the tender regions of the heart. An entire house can be transformed into a temple of reverence for the myriad feelings, memories, and interactions that constitute our lives. In the following pages I would like to suggest ways for you to make sacred places of your own, steps that can help you transform your immediate environment in ways that nurture the totality of who you are. Innumerable paths to integrate mind, body, and surroundings in a rich blend of wholeness present themselves, but I will discuss five commonly shared stages of bringing consciousness into physical form: vision, seed conception, planning, craft, and ritual.

VISION

He carried me away . . . and showed me that great city . . .
descending out of heaven from God . . . and her light was
like unto a stone most precious . . . clear as crystal; And had
a wall great and high, and had twelve gates, and at the gates
twelve angels. . . . On the east three gates; on the north
three gates; on the south three gates; and on the west three
gates. And the wall of the city had twelve foundations. . . .
And he that talked with me had a golden reed to measure the
city. . . . And the city lieth foursquare. . . . And the building of the wall of it was of jasper: and the city was pure gold,
like unto clear glass. And the foundations of the wall were
garnished with all manner of precious stones. **Revelation**

Vision is the flow of consciousness into luminous images that res-
onate with personal significance. The spontaneous wisdom of dreams
and flashes of insight reveal the shape of the psyche as it takes tangible form. Within each of us sparkles a vision of a personal sacred
place. It may only be a faint glimmer of feeling hidden beneath layers
of daily concerns, but that inner spark is glowing, waiting to be
stoked. With care and attention, we can open our awareness to the
shimmering forms that reflect the design of the soul.

Envisioning a Personal Sacred Place

The following exploration provides a means of discovering a vision of
a personal sacred place. As you move through the process allow your
heart and mind to go where they will. As Saint Teresa of Ávila explained, "The soul is capable of much more than we can imagine,
[and it is] very important for the soul . . . not to hold itself back and
stay in one corner. Let it walk through dwelling places which are up
above, down below, and to the sides, since God has given it great dignity." During the process, set aside any preconceived notions of what
a sacred place "should" be, simply observing the images and feelings
as they arise. Let go of judgments about the practicality or cost of the
sacred place you envision. (Ways of making your vision a concrete reality will be discussed in this chapter in the section on planning.) Allow yourself to deeply feel the impulses of consciousness as they rise
within you. If the images seem faint, enjoy their subtlety; don't try to

*Only in a hut
built for the moment can
one live without fears.*
Kamo no Chomei

*Whosoever builds for
God a place of worship, be it
only as the nest of a grouse,
Allah builds for him a house
in paradise.*
Mohammed

What you see you become.
Vedic proverb

bring them into sharper focus. Allow the images that naturally present themselves to fill your consciousness. Give yourself an opportunity to find the sacred place within you.

Locate a calm, quiet spot where you can go through the following exploration without being disturbed. Have a friend read the sentences to you, pausing sufficiently between each one to allow your imagination time for a thorough experience. You can also read them into a tape recorder and play them back to yourself at a leisurely pace.

*Architecture is born
in the heart.*
Frank Lloyd Wright

From joy springs all creation.
Mundaka Upanishad

*We could decorate our homes
with images from our dreams
and waking fantasy.*
Thomas Moore

- Sit in a comfortable position and close your eyes. Allow your attention to settle into the rhythm of your breathing. Feel the easy flow of air, in and out, in and out.

- Allow your attention to go to your heart. Experience the feeling you find there. Let go of any thoughts you have about the feeling, just settle into it. Experience its depth and subtle nuances.

- Imagine a floor supporting this feeling. What are the qualities of this floor? Is it raised, lowered, or level with the surroundings? What is its shape? Is it round, square, octagonal, or of some other design? Of what is the floor made? See its color and pattern.

- Imagine the walls that shelter this feeling. Are they massive and solid or light and transparent? Are pillars used in place of walls? How tall are the walls or pillars? Of what are they made? Do they have a specific color or pattern?

- Imagine the roof that shelters the feeling. What is the shape of this roof? Is it domed, peaked, or flat? Of what is it made? Does it have a specific color or pattern?

- Imagine the doors and windows that allow the feeling to flow out into the world. How many doors and windows are there? Where are they located? What are their sizes and shapes? Of what are they made? See their colors and textures.

- Imagine the ornamentation that expresses the feeling. What is the treatment around the doors and windows? Are there paintings or other forms of decoration on the walls, ceiling, or floor?

- Imagine the quality of light that reflects the feeling. What is the source of this light? Is it the sun, moon, stars, candles, or electric light? Is there lighting for special tasks?

■ Imagine the sounds that echo the feeling. Envision the textures, colors, tastes, and aromas that have those qualities. How does the place that supports and shelters this feeling change from morning to afternoon to evening? In winter, spring, summer, and autumn?

■ Are there any other qualities or features you would like to add that express the feeling?

■ Sit quietly for a while, enjoying the sacred place you have envisioned. Feel what it is like to inhabit a room or garden that cares for your soul. Imagine what you will do in your sacred place. Will you meditate, read, play music, draw, or engage in a specific spiritual practice?

■ When you feel ready to leave this sacred place, open your eyes slowly and recall what you experienced. Draw and write about your impressions on a piece of paper. Continue to let your imagination flow around the feeling in your heart, filling in any new details that come to you. Over the coming days and weeks refer to these pictures and comments, adding or subtracting the qualities that feel right to you. Review the previous chapters of this book, seeing if you find the archetypal patterns they describe reflected in your own sacred place. Does it incorporate gate, path, and lotus seat, steeple and sanctuary, the body's form and function, and a relationship to sunlight?

The artist must attune himself to that which wants to reveal itself and permit the process to happen through him.
Martin Heidegger

Some are endowed with the ability to reconstruct the entire universe by knowing a blade of grass.
Louis Kahn

SEED CONCEPTION

The process of making a sacred place involves many choices. Locating a central reference point that integrates diverse forms, materials, colors, and other design elements is a helpful technique for creating a place of wholeness. This reference point is a seed concept. When we describe the specific quality of a place, we define its seed concept, its central feeling. That of an intimate cottage differs from that of a stately mansion. The notion of moving from coziness to expansion provides a nucleus that supports the contrast between these two qualities of experience and heightens the identity of each.

The variety of seed concepts is probably endless. Every quality of consciousness has a corresponding form that can be identified and used as a central idea. They all, however, share the common characteristic of expressing the movement of thought and feeling within us.

149

Seed concepts can be derived from qualities of light, such as moving from darkness to brilliance, or from variations on a particular color. They can express relationships of geometry—modifications of a square, circle, or graceful curve. Sacred places can be designed around a feature in the natural landscape, like a tree, rock, or stream.

In the guided visualization above, you discovered the qualities of consciousness that define your personal sacred place. The first step in moving from abstract thoughts and feelings to a tangible environment is the formation of a seed concept. This essential idea is given shape in a seed diagram, a visual symbol that expresses the central feelings of your vision. A seed diagram is a simple collection of lines that captures the essential qualities of the heart that you want to shelter and support. This diagram can provide a referral point for all the choices that inform a sacred place.

A seed concept diagram of a central core of light surrounded by layers of enclosure (top). The next diagram shows the fanning out of consciousness from a point to a field. Moving through darkness to light is next. A fluid dance through an orderly field of light is shown at the bottom.

Making a Seed Diagram

To develop a seed concept for making your sacred place, try the following exploration.

- Sit easily, with your eyes closed, and go back to the personal vision of the sacred place you discovered in the last exploration. Allow yourself to spend some time remembering and feeling the qualities of experience you found in that vision. When you feel settled into those qualities of experience, say to yourself, "My sacred place is a _____ place," using one or more words that characterize your vision. Be aware of the feelings and thoughts that arise within you. Your first response might be a physical sensation such as warmth, energy, or relaxation. It could be a visual image of a geometric shape, a color, or a place in the recesses of your memory. A word such as "ever-expanding" or "womblike" or a phrase may spring to mind. Whatever happens, allow yourself to savor the feeling you experience.

- Open your eyes and write down the word or phrase that sums up your feelings. This is the seed concept of your personal house.

- To discover the visual shape that embodies the central feeling of your sacred place, write the following sentence on a piece of paper, "My sacred place is a _____ place and is expressed by the shape(s) of a _____." Draw this shape. It could be a circle, square, triangle, squiggle, or any other form that expresses your seed concept's particular characteristics.

Whether you think you can draw or not, just move the pencil across the paper in a way that expresses the feeling of the sacred place within you. This is only for yourself, you don't have to show it to anyone. You may get even better results with your eyes closed. The intention here is to translate abstract feelings into the first sprouting of form. If this seems unclear, refer to the illustration of theme diagrams. Keep drawing until you have created a diagram that you feel truly expresses your theme.

You have just drawn the seed diagram of your sacred place. Feel free to redraw it, adding clarification or richness. Let what you have created sit for a couple of days and see what develops. You may gain some new insights into your seed concept that refine your diagram in some way. In the next section we will use your seed diagram as a basis for planning all the details of your sacred place.

PLANNING

Visions of a sacred place and the seed concepts that distill the essence of those visions are abstract by nature. They are intimate stirrings of the heart, initial gestures that bring a tangible place of wholeness into being. From these awakenings comes a plan diagram. Developing a plan diagram is a procedure of specifying the particular attributes of a sacred place. The actions that occur there and qualities of consciousness experienced within are given definition and scale. The plan diagram describes a sacred place's qualities of enclosure. It clarifies the arrangement of gate, path, and lotus seat, develops the shapes of the steeple and sanctuary, and marks the alignment with nature's patterns of renewal. The specific characteristics of form and space that respond to the core of your being are clarified.

You can begin planning your sacred place by choosing where it will be located within your house or garden. It might be a room set aside for spiritual practices, a nook, patio, or porch. If possible, clear everything out of this place so you can begin with a clean slate. Go through the sentences below to discover how you might transform your vision of the sacred into a concrete reality. Imagine the ways you might turn the various aspects of your vision into tangible materials given the time and money available to you. Have the seed concept diagram you created above by your side. As you design the different

Integrity is the deepest quality in a building.
Frank Lloyd Wright

The vessel in which soulmaking takes place is an inner container scooped out by reflection and wonder.
Thomas Moore

151

aspects of your sacred place, see how they refer to the seed concept. Throughout this process allow your thinking and feeling to be flexible. As each new piece of the puzzle is added, the other pieces may have to be adjusted so they fit together harmoniously. An arrangement that is too rigid can stifle your spirit, as the tea master Rikyu once demonstrated.

One day Rikyu asked his son Do-an to clean the path leading through the tea garden. Do-an swept and scrubbed each stepping-stone with the greatest of care and then asked his father to inspect the work. "Not complete," was the master's response. Again Do-an engaged in the task with even greater mindfulness until each speck of dust and pine needle was washed away. He called his father a second time to look over his work and again it was not accepted. After a third cleaning, Do-an was certain that the path was in perfect condition, but Rikyu just shook his head. In desperation the son threw up his hands and shouted, "Well, you show me how to do it then!" The tea master walked to a maple tree near the path, grabbed the trunk, and gave it a vigorous shake. A rain of autumn leaves sprinkled the path with an array of dazzling colors. "Now the garden is perfect," he said.

When you have all the answers about a building before you start building it, your answers are not true. The building gives you answers as it grows and becomes itself.
Louis Kahn

We shape our buildings; thereafter they shape us.
Winston Churchill

Making a Plan Diagram

- Sit quietly in the place you have chosen and recall your vision. Remember the core feeling of your sacred place. Think of what you will do there.

- Take out your seed concept diagram and see how it pertains to the feeling in your heart. Does the shape of the diagram relate to the area where you will make your sacred place? How could the room or garden be altered to reflect the diagram?

- Remember the floor of your vision. How could you make the floor you are sitting on like the one you imagined? How will it support what you do there? If you envisioned a floor of costly materials or elaborate design, think of ways to create the same qualities of texture, color, shape, and pattern within your means.

- Recall the walls and/or pillars that sheltered the core feeling in your heart. How could you construct similar structures in this area? How will they shelter what you do in your sacred place? Are there ways you might echo the massive or transparent feeling of the walls or pillars in your vision?

- Bring to mind the ceiling of your vision. Imagine the ways you might shape a roof like that with fabric or some other easily worked material.

- Remember the doors and windows that helped to define your vision. See how you could create gateways and windows that give a similar feeling. Maybe a mural or painting on the wall could serve a similar purpose. Imagine how you might define the threshold crossing into your sacred place.

- Recall the ornamentation and decoration of your vision. In what ways could you express that treatment around the doors and windows or on the walls, ceiling, and floor?

- Bring to mind the quality of light that reflects the feeling in your heart. How might you use light fixtures or candles to reproduce that quality of illumination? Imagine the light at different times of the day and seasons of the year. Are there ways that you could honor the cycles of the sun, moon, and stars in the sacred place you are creating?

- Remember the sounds, textures, colors, tastes, and aromas of your vision. Think of ways to make them tangible experiences in your room or garden.

- Add any other qualities or features that express the feeling in your heart.

- Sit quietly for a while, enjoying the plan of your sacred place. Feel what it would be like to inhabit that room or garden. Will you want any special furniture or equipment to support what you will do there?

- Draw and write about your impressions. Continue to let your imagination flow around the recollections of your vision, filling in any new details that come to you. Draw everything in as much detail as possible, getting into the subtle nuances, forms, and textures of your sacred place. See if your sacred place incorporates the fundamental patterns of gate, path, and lotus seat, steeple and sanctuary, the body's form and function, and a relationship to sunlight.

When I am working on a problem, I never think about beauty. I think only how to solve the problem. But when I have finished, if the solution is not beautiful, I know it is wrong.
Buckminster Fuller

Go to the woods and fields for color schemes.
Frank Lloyd Wright

153

CRAFT

In Chapter One, I discussed how every object begins as a thought in someone's mind, how our inner processes lead us to gather materials and shape them into the walls, furnishings, and other forms that define our living environments. This process of transformation is called craft. Making a tangible home for the soul is the essence of crafting a sacred place.

At its essence, craft is a dialogue with the materials and objects that surround us. The motions of the hand whisper the desires of the heart in a language that wood, stone, fabric, and other substances can understand. Craftspeople listen carefully to the materials they work with in order to discover the shapes and uses for which those substances are best suited. They go beyond simply molding stuff, imparting spirit to the objects they create. The architect Charles Moore once said that the more energy a person puts into a building, the more he or she receives from it.

Most of us have experienced places that are enhanced by craft—a home whose stair rail receives the hand with ease, or whose entry is especially welcoming. There is something about such places that goes beyond a mere appreciation of their parts. We sense the hands and mind of a craftsperson at work; a nurturing wholeness pervades the atmosphere.

The Arts and Crafts movement, spearheaded in the last century by William Morris, encouraged this approach in designing buildings and creating commonplace objects. Morris believed that craft was "the way in which man expresses joy in his work." He went on to say that "architecture embraces the consideration of the whole external surroundings of the life of man . . . 'tis we ourselves, each one of us, who must keep watch over the fairness of the earth, and each with his soul and hand do his share therein." Arts and Crafts designers found the sacred in everyday things, in wood grain, the colors of nature, and plant forms. Architects such as Greene and Greene, Frank Lloyd Wright, and Gustav Stickley designed homes and furnishings that displayed the intimate relationship between the soul, the hand, and architecture.

The tools that serve the varied functions of craft can express the link between spirit and matter. In the Masonic tradition, the Working Tools signify qualities of consciousness that the craftsperson must identify, infuse into heart and mind, and then use in daily life. A

The joinery of a staircase detail by Greene and Greene records the meeting of consciousness and matter. The craftsperson's thoughts are chiseled into the rounded corners, pegged connectors, and other nuances of craft (opposite).

The chief characteristic of handicrafts is that they maintain by their very nature a direct link with the human heart.
Soetsu Yanagi

hammer, for example, is an active tool of force, associated with passion, joy, rage, and commitment. A chisel, on the other hand, is a passive, containing tool; it receives the blows of the hammer and directs them with precision. A chisel can be equated with the mind's ability to analyze, classify, calculate, and think rationally. The ruler provides the measurements that hold the hammer and chisel in balance. Tools such as the level, the plumb line, and the square are implements of testing in relation to an absolute criterion. The level measures in reference to absolute horizontality. It expresses balance, passivity, stillness, somberness, constraint, discipline, and support. The plumb line measures in relation to absolute verticality. Its surrender to the force of gravity can be seen as corresponding to giving, generosity, and mercy. Through surrender, the plumb line locates the midpoint of the world. Wherever we stand on the globe's surface, gravity pulls the plumb line toward the center of the earth. The square, like the measuring tape, defines the relationship between the level and the plumb line. The pencil and the compass are tools of design and creativity. The pencil brings the initial sproutings of the craftsperson's consciousness into the physical world. The compass guides this flow of energy and intelligence; the creative energy of the moving point of the tool becomes harmonious through its connection to the stationary point planted firmly in the drawing surface. Design ideas expand without losing contact with their unmoving, infinite source.

Angel Quilpe, a Tipai man, lashes together the poles of a grass-house frame. Joining materials through crossing employs an archetypal principle—creation arises by the overlapping of opposites. Male/female, firm/yielding, heaven/earth, and other polarities join to spawn new offspring.

Crafting a Sacred Place

- Making a sacred place provides an opportunity to experience the transforming power of craft. As you gather materials and begin arranging them to define a sacred area of your home or garden, notice the connections between your thoughts and the way your body moves. Is your mind going in an opposite direction from that of your body? If it is, let your awareness settle into the flow of energy that guides the movements of your hands and notice the difference.

- See what connections you can make between your thoughts, actions, and the patterns of intelligence in the materials you are working with. If you are sanding and finishing wood, notice the effect your actions have on the material. Pause to feel its texture, smell its aroma, and hear the sound that the wood makes. Listen to what the material might be telling you. While crafting the floor of your sacred place, let yourself get in touch with the consciousness of "floorness." Do this with each element, discovering the awareness of "wallness," "windowness," etc. If you are creating a sacred garden, see if you can find the kinship between the plants you are placing in the earth and the core feeling in your heart.

- Notice the different qualities of consciousness expressed by oak and pine, cotton and silk, roses and lilies, and other materials. Imagine the creative ways you can use a material or the unexpected materials you might employ. Could highly polished wood be used in place of marble or granite? Would rice paper on a wooden frame provide a subtle alternative to building a two-by-four–and–plasterboard wall?

- Go at an easy pace and take this opportunity to create something that is deeply satisfying. Imagine how wonderful the rest of your home or workplace would be if every form and space within it was created from this integrated quality of mind, body, and surroundings.

RITUAL

Sacredness is not a static thing, done once and for all. The process of making a sacred place continues to unfold over time. The spirit of the place is rekindled by actions that revitalize mind, body, and environment. These renewing actions are called rituals.

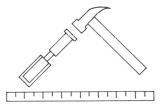

Hammer, chisel, and ruler.

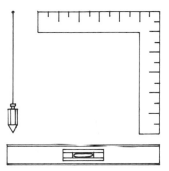

Plumb bob, level, and square.

Compass and pencil.

The Working Tools of the Masonic tradition are symbols of sacred craft. Each tool represents a different nuance of the soul.

157

Marking the sacred times and places of our existence, rituals help us to feel the movement of inner spirit, to experience inner and outer realms flowing together in a common stream. Setting aside a regular time for meditation, prayer, or creative pursuits, or simply lighting a candle, writing about an intimate experience, or fixing a meal begins a cycle of opening mind and body to the revitalizing powers of the soul. Here the rifts within us can be healed and the pulse of our creative energies can be felt.

In the Japanese tea ceremony, for example, the mere act of making a cup of tea becomes a magical experience. A number of years ago I learned an informal version of this ceremony, which is performed in the following manner. A wooden plank set on the floor serves as a table. On it are placed an earthenware jug, a tea bowl, and a waste-water jar. A bamboo dipper, tea scoop, and whisk act as utensils. The

A few bowls and bamboo utensils create a sacred place where the fluid craft of making a cup of tea can be savored.

tea is held in a small container called a caddy. Earthy tones tint the clay vessels; a variety of textures invites the touch of the hand. Server and guests are seated on cushions around the table. This simple arrangement seems to induce a quiet alertness.

The ceremony begins when the server lifts the lid from the jug. Steam rises from the heated waters within. A deeply satisfying *kerplunk* sounds as the dipper is thrust into the sparkling liquid, like a stone dropping into the still waters of a pond. A dipperful is poured into the tea bowl, stirred with the bamboo whisk, and emptied from the tea bowl into the wastewater jar. The tea bowl is wiped clean with a cloth. The caddy is then opened, unveiling the shockingly bright acid green of the powdered tea; a faint mist of tea dust momentarily hovers above the caddy. With a small bamboo scoop, shaped somewhat like a snow ski, two scoopfuls of powder are dropped into the tea bowl. A sharp tap of the scoop on the edge of the bowl knocks the remaining grains of tea free. Two dipperfuls of water gurgle into the bowl. Several quick flicks of the bamboo whisk whip the ingredients into a frothy mixture, a green sea foam of glistening bubbles. The bowl is passed to the guest on the server's left with a bow. After savoring the tea's warmth and aroma, the first guest takes a few sips and then passes the bowl to the next person. The bowl makes its way around the circle until it is returned to the server. In the same careful way that the tea was made, the server mindfully washes the empty vessel. A dipperful of water, the swish of the whisk, a swipe of the cloth, and it is done. The bamboo utensils and earthenware vessels are returned to their original position. The lid of the water jug is replaced with a clink.

The sacredness of the simplest acts shines forth in this little ritual. Pausing to give attention to an ordinary cup of tea, the miraculous connection of mind, body, and object becomes apparent. The dexterity of the hand in performing the various tasks is coupled with the subtle abilities of the senses to perceive the nuances of sound, texture, light, taste, and smell. The table offers a microcosm of the natural world. A steam cloud rising from the jug, a river of water from the dipper, an ocean of frothy tea, the earthy solidity of the clay bowls, the floral delicacy of the bamboo utensils, and the vital power of the ground tea leaves all blend in the cyclical processes of creation, maintenance, and dissolution. The communion of a shared intimacy is blessed by simple appreciation.

What, then, did the Tea masters see—what did their vision disclose? It was the reflection of the inner nature of things, the reality of things, which the old philosophers called "the eternal mode." They saw the thing itself, the whole which is entirely different from the sum of its parts.
Soetsu Yanagi

The pot shows the universe.
Bengali proverb

Establishing a Sacred Ritual

- Your sacred place is an outer form that reflects the patterns of consciousness within you. Look at what you have created and see what activities or modes of experience are suggested by the design. A soaring space might invite you to dance. Wonderful acoustics could inspire singing. A window with a garden view may frame a place to silently witness the processes of nature.

- Use your sacred place in ways that are personal to you. Establish a regular time to let the world go and turn your consciousness back on yourself. Enjoy the freedom to get in touch with who you really are and how you want to live. Rearrange or add to your sacred place as the spirit moves you. Make it a setting where you can be who you want to be, a place where you learn to feel the presence of the sacred in a tangible way.

Twin pillars define an entry hall that is bathed with light from above (opposite).

Care of the soul requires a special crafting of life itself, with an artist's sensitivity to the way things are done.
Thomas Moore

Food, a gift of the earth, is honored in this dining area that recalls a church.

A wreath and angel make a wall a sacred place.

A place like this [garden] is a device that takes you from the world you are actually living in and removes you. It was designed to create a mood, to bring one into a poetic state of mind.
Makoto Ooka

A garden bench at Dumbarton Oaks provides a lotus seat.

The workings of the soul don't need to be confined to one sacred place. Vision, seed conception, planning, craft, and ritual can be extended to all areas of the physical environment. With care and attention, every room can become a sacred place. In his book *In Praise of Shadows*, Junichiro Tanizaki likened the qualities of the traditional Japanese toilet to a shrine:

> The parlor may have its charms, but the Japanese toilet is truly a place of spiritual repose. . . . No words can describe that sensation as one sits in the dim light, basking in the faint glow reflected in the shoji, lost in meditation or gazing out at the garden. . . . I love to listen from such a toilet to the sound of softly falling rain. . . . And the toilet is the perfect place to listen to the chirping of insects or the song of birds, to view the moon, or to enjoy the poignant moments that mark the change of the seasons. Here, I suspect, is the place where haiku poets over the ages have come by a great many of their ideas. . . . Our forebears, making poetry of everything in their lives, transformed what should be the most unsanitary room in the house into a place of unsurpassed elegance, replete with fond associations with the beauties of nature.

Seeing and Creating

1. The simplest, most direct method of creating sacredness into everyday surroundings is cleaning. I know this activity is usually relegated to the realm of drudgery, but it can become a practical means of infusing consciousness into your surroundings. Sacredness is experienced in the qualities of purity, orderliness, balance, and renewal. All of these are achieved through cleaning. In the process, neglected objects and corners of our living environments receive love and attention. The glow of consciousness passes into floors, furniture, dishes, and countertops, making them shine. Without spending a penny on redesign, the room is transformed.

2. Use the process of vision, seed conception, planning, craft, and ritual to transform the everyday rooms you take for granted. See how each aspect of your physical surroundings could be shaped to reflect the subtle shadings of sacredness. For example, think of how the kitchen's floor, walls, cabinets, etc. might support and nurture the core feeling in your heart. Do this room by room to create a living environment that cares for the wholeness of your soul.

3. Extend this process to the place where you work. Your desk could be seen as a microcosm of the mythological forces that shape the universe; certainly the warriorlike energies of Mars, the wisdom of Jupiter, the creative power of the sun, and the volatile energies of Mercury shape the story of every business day. Through imagination and care, the soul could be enlivened in every bit of the environment, making your world a sacred place.

4. Apply the above process to a garden. Find plants whose shape, color, texture, and fragrance express the various aspects of your personality—hope, fear, strength, insight, vulnerability, etc. Imagine how each personality trait might relate to and support the others, and place the plants in that arrangement. Use your cultivation of the garden as a means of tending to the sprouting, growth, and transformation of your consciousness.

EIGHT

The Sacred City

Meet together, speak together, let your minds be functioning
from a common source. . . .
Common be your prayer, common the purpose,
associated the desire. . . .
Common be the wishes of your hearts; common be your thoughts,
so that there be thorough union among you.

RIG VEDA

The solitude of personal sacred places extends to encompass the shared consciousness of community. Whether we dwell in the remote realm of a mountain cave or the secluded room of an inner-city apartment, each of us is linked to a far-reaching system of human aspirations and deeds. The clothes we wear, the food we eat, and the buildings that shelter us are produced by a vast network of individuals who join forces to fulfill the needs of our larger self in society. Even our modes of perceiving the world are part of the culture in which we live. The monk who physically "leaves the world" carries with him a bulky collection of cultural baggage, a burden that may make for a difficult passage through the gates of limited thinking into the land of spirit.

Besides, going on retreat is only a phase of the spiritual quest. The individual seeking to liberate the full powers of his or her consciousness truly finds fulfillment in the return to the gathering circle of community, where the treasures of wisdom can be shared. Moses returned with the Ten Commandments, Buddha with the Eightfold Path, Shankara with the Crest Jewel of Wisdom. The stage at which Buddha meditated under the tree is not the ultimate goal of the spiritual journey. It may be a necessary step, but it is not the end of the path. The aim is to realize that the essence of oneself and the essence of the world, which appear to be separate, are actually two expressions of one underlying field of consciousness. Through social participation, an individual's awareness is opened to the self in the all and the all in the self.

See the world as your self.
Have faith in the way things are.
Love the world as your self;
then you can care for all things.
Tao te Ching

The search for the sacred in commonplace architecture leads to the streets and buildings of urban life. Unless the pulse of the soul can be found beating at the heart of the city, there will be limits to the sacredness that can be found in everyday life. In a more hopeful era, Louis Kahn called the city a "place where a small boy, as he walks through it, may see something that will tell him what he wants to do his whole life." But these are different times. Crime, violence, homelessness, pollution, and a crumbling infrastructure plague our communities. Fear and alienation have become dominant factors in shaping the social, economic, and environmental quality of the city. It seems that boys and girls need their fair share of savvy and street smarts just to survive, let alone think of what they want to do their whole life. Faced with the harsh reality of these problems, most of us turn inward, searching for a nurturing wholeness within the limited circle of ourselves, our family, and our friends.

Yet we know that this is a temporary solution at best. For deep within us is the feeling that the health and well-being of our own existence is intimately yoked to the common good of the greater human family. One of the many elements that link each of us to this larger whole is the architecture of cities and towns. Goods and services arrive at our doors through a network of highways and streets. Talents and abilities are exchanged within the walls of offices, factories, and stores. Schools and centers for the arts pass knowledge and culture

Schools began with a man under a tree, who did not know he was a teacher, discussing his realization with a few, who did not know they were students. The students aspired that their sons also listen to such a man. Spaces were erected and the first schools became. It can also be said that the existence-will of school was there even before the circumstances of the man under the tree.
Louis Kahn

from one generation to the next. Strength and heroism are cheered in the gathering bowls of stadiums and sports arenas.

Architecture shelters the soul of community and influences the shape of its expression in the world. Certainly the urban problems we face were not caused by urban planning, nor can they be solved by it. Simply redesigning a city will not heal the hearts and minds of those who inhabit it. Architecture can, however, offer a window onto the ways our shared consciousness shapes the experience of community life. Because buildings, plazas, and streets are the outcome of human thought and action, they can show us the genuine condition of society's mind—acting as indicators of the strength, or frailty, of the collective soul. When attuned to the specific needs and desires of that common spirit, architecture becomes a tool for integrating and nurturing private needs and public endeavors.

One cannot settle in the world without assuming the responsibility to create it.
Mircea Eliade

COLLECTIVE MIND, COLLECTIVE BODY

The city is the body of collective consciousness. Just as a house reflects its occupants—windows serving as eyes and air passages, siding as skin, plumbing as veins, the kitchen as a stomach—cities extend the heart and mind of a community into the infrastructure of its streets, services, and buildings. When the soul of a people is wounded, the physical body of the city is injured; when it is healthy, urban life flourishes. The diseases that plague modern society find direct expression in the city's architecture. Collective consciousness is now afflicted by fragmentation, depression, violence, isolation, loss of memory, numbness, and emptiness. When traveling through most urban environments, you will see these symptoms everywhere. The jarring cacophony of street sounds echoes the hard, fragmented, and angry inner life of many city dwellers. Automobile-encapsulated citizens can see an expression of their own isolation, emptiness, and lack of a historic sense of place in the glass-and-steel monoliths that edge city boulevards. For the most part, modern office towers, public buildings, and shopping malls exhibit a monotony and lack of detail that reveal the inner emptiness that characterizes much of modern life.

As Robert Sardello points out in *Facing the World with Soul*, skyscrapers dominate the city. Their soaring shapes may act as spectacular, dazzling, and powerful steeples, but they are undeniably cold and unfeeling. With taut, glassy skins and sharp lines, they display the anorexia of urban consciousness, the lack of nourishing sensory experience. Skyscrapers, he believes, are manifestations of a self-centered ego—designs that turn architecture into "egotecture" and create a wasteland of hollow, inflated, monotonous, lonely, and defiant spaces. Flashy on the outside, these buildings provide interior spaces that are nothing more than glorified filing cabinets. Endless housing developments, Sardello goes on to say, are no more than skyscrapers laid on their sides.

In essence, a city's problems are fundamentally problems in consciousness. In the year 500, the Byzantine historian Procopius, writing about violence in the large cities of the Eastern Roman Empire, said, "I for my part can only call this a disease of the soul." Homelessness expresses the rootlessness we feel in our hearts. Homeless people embody shattered connections between mind, body, and

In the field of art, each country tends to produce a kind of art which somehow reflects national characteristics.
Aaron Copland

The strength of a nation is derived from the integrity of its homes.
Confucius

environment. This is not just a problem of alienation among people, but a breakdown of integration between our thoughts, actions, and the places we inhabit. This split between consciousness and matter separates people from the material comforts of houses, schools, and workplaces. Crime reveals the internal emptiness that motivates needy acts of greed and selfishness. Violence displays our emotional rage and feelings of powerlessness. Pollution is the toxic effect of self-hatred, spawning ways of living that ravage the ecological systems essential to human existence.

Contemporary cities are not designed to care for people. Instead of nurturing health and well-being, they are settings that favor alienation and violence. This conflict discourages people from caring for the very urban structures that house them. The body of the city continues to die; the soul of the community continues to wither. Medicine, education, agriculture, business, art, religion, and other shared expressions of the human spirit have lost their power to enrich our culture. A paralysis has spread across the city.

Lower Manhattan seems to rise from the water, reflecting the notion of the city rising out of collective consciousness. Each building can be seen as expressing a particular quality of the communal spirit.

Significant revitalization can only begin when we look beyond surface disorders and learn to care for society's soul—reawakening the consciousness that animates the deepest needs and aspirations of the community. Initial steps in this direction are taken when the stirrings of individual hearts and minds are connected to the environments close at hand, to homes and workplaces. By following the natural extension of the human spirit through these personal places into the world, we can discover the relationship between collective consciousness and its physical manifestation in urban architecture. In the process, the city's sacredness can be realized. This journey passes through seven basic elements of community: money, facets of totality, society and solitude, the silent hub, regeneration, and new patterns of unity.

The prosperity of a country depends not on the abundance of its revenues, nor on the strength of its fortifications, nor on the beauty of its public buildings; but consists in the number of its cultivated citizens, in [those of] education, enlightenment, and character; here are found its true interest, its chief strength, its real power.
Martin Luther

MONEY
When rich speculators prosper while farmers lose their land;
when government officials spend money on weapons instead of cures;
when the upper class is extravagant and irresponsible
while the poor have nowhere to turn—all this is robbery and chaos.
It is not in keeping with the Tao.

Tao te Ching

The templelike design of the Lincoln Memorial on the back of a penny indicates the sacred qualities that a society can associate with money.

The city is where shared notions of time, size, weight, and other values are developed; it is the place of measure. The city is an outward measure of human achievement through technology as well as an inner measure of consciousness through art, knowledge, and sacred places. Money not only buys the building blocks of architecture, it also drives the affairs of a city. How a city spends its money is a reflection of the richness or poverty of its inner life. When money becomes the measure of a city, we are no longer able to remember the value of life. When money is given greater value than human communication and ecological health, the body of the city is wounded by homelessness, crime, drugs, and pollution. Lavishing more money and attention on the architecture of banks and office buildings than on that of schools, art centers, and houses of worship indicates a distorted balance of value in the city. Unless shelter and support are provided for every aspect of community, the fragile well-being of the marketplace is thrown off and the healing powers of the city's soul are frustrated. The transformation of the soul's pain into the inward silver and gold of awakened consciousness is the genuine purpose of exchange in the marketplace. This is the true spiritual alchemy of commerce, art, and culture.

To envision a city that balances and enriches the inner and outer dimensions of community is to perceive the harmonic workings of the one in the many. It is the art of seeing the diverse shapes and purposes of the urban landscape as a celebration of the sacredness of each individual and of the meeting places that join their diversity. The social rites of birth, initiation, marriage, and burial translate human lives into timeless, prototypic forms. They reveal the shape of one's consciousness, not as this or that personality, but as the archetypes of the chief, mother, father, healer, builder, or merchant. Everyone participates in the community according to the needs of his or her soul, and the whole society gains the self-awakened vision of an imperishable living unit. Generations of individuals pass, like the cells of a living body, but the sustaining timeless form of the community remains. By expanding one's vision to embrace the whole, each citizen is enhanced, enriched, supported, and magnified.

The city's architecture is an active participant in this play of consciousness. Market, theater, church, school, hospital, council hall, workplace, and plaza each embody a distinct character that works to nurture the varied facets of totality. Every institution strives to display in physical form a different inflection of the community's soul—insight in the school, loving care in the hospital, delightful illusion at the theater. These diverse expressions externalize the spirit of the culture and make concrete the memory of its evolution.

The kind of work we do does not make us holy but we make it holy.
Meister Eckhart

Happiness lies not in the mere possession of money; it lies in the enjoyment of achievement, the thrill of creative effort.
Franklin D. Roosevelt

A relief of construction workers adorns the crossbeam of the Federal Trade Commission Building.

171

The light-filled hallway of a hospital in Paris encourages healing by uplifting the human spirit (right). The Mississauga Civic Centre by Jones & Kirkland combines urban and rural forms to create a focus for an aspiring city (opposite).

SOCIETY AND SOLITUDE

Shaping the city's design is a fundamental pattern of consciousness—the gradation of experience from communal gathering to personal solitude. Urban architecture's essential purpose is to provide settings for the full range of human experience. Walking through the small midwestern town where I live, I find a clear example of this organizing principle. The town square at the center acts as a kind of public living room, the gathering place for political rallies, concerts, Fourth of July festivities, and tributes to those who died in foreign wars. On hot August days, people collect in small groups beneath the square's spreading maple trees; here the cooling shade and breezes offer a common haven for playing cards, listening to a baseball game on the radio, or adding to the communal history through news and gossip. Ringing the square are businesses that serve the town's varied needs: clothing stores, gift shops, and restaurants, a market, drugstore, bank, hair salon, barbershop, portrait studio, TV-and-appliance store, hardware store, furniture store, movie house, attorney's office, computer center, and others. Just outside the central ring of commerce are government and religious buildings: the library, courthouse, post office, church, and city hall. The grid of streets and sidewalks links the public realm to the private domain of family homes. Even here, the gradation of experience from community to solitude shapes the architecture. Covered porches create outdoor rooms where public and private overlap. Living and dining rooms provide more secluded, yet social, places of interaction. Bedrooms on the upper floors complete the range of possibilities by cradling the most intimate of experiences. Layer upon layer of enclosure supports the full spectrum of consciousness.

THE SILENT HUB

Louis Kahn called the city "the place of availabilities." "A plan," he continued, "is a society of rooms. The plan of a city is no more complex than the plan of a house." He said that the city isn't a grouping of systems, but has an essential nature that must be respected. This nature is the sense of commonality, the natural agreement among people. The street is the architectural manifestation of this sense of commonality. Kahn called the street "a room by agreement, a community room, the walls of which belong to the donors, dedicated to the city for common use." It organizes the city by providing a space where collective consciousness can gather and direct its energies.

The time of business does not with me differ from the time of prayer, and in the noise and clatter of my kitchen, while several persons are calling for different things, I possess God in as great tranquillity as if I were upon my knees at the Blessed Sacrament.
Brother Lawrence

No wonder so many early settlements came into existence at the intersection of two roads. Here the mythic image of the universe emanating from a central point and spreading to the four directions of space is brought to earth, organizing human existence. The perpendicular lines of these two intersecting streets generated a square that became a fundamental model in urban planning. Cities in China, India, Persia, Greece, and Rome as well as in North and South America are based on this archetype.

New York's Central Park provides an empty core for the city's diverse activities, a place for citizens to reconnect with nature and perhaps find a moment of solitude.

The sense of mystery, the gratitude for being alive, the sense of transcendent energy that unites all of us, coordinates our cities, coordinates our lives.

Joseph Campbell

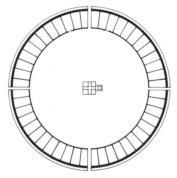

The original city of Baghdad marked the high point of circular cities in the Middle East. The mosque and palace established the center, while residential neighborhoods ringed the perimeter, an endeavor to balance individual and community needs.

Often a space was left empty in the center of this idealized plan. At these plazas, commons, and squares, the commonality expressed in each street touched the nerve center of the collective mind. Like the wheel that turns by joining spokes at an empty hub, the city was animated by joining streets around a central plaza.

Circular layouts form another archetype of city design. The Persian city of Ecbatana, built in 715 B.C., was defined by a series of concentric walls. Each successive circle was higher than the one below it. There were seven circles in all, with the palace and treasury at the center. The battlements of the five outer rings were painted different colors; the outermost circle was white, then followed black, red, blue, and orange. The two inner walls were plated with silver and gold, respectively. Each layer of enclosure symbolized a different level of spiritual realization, starting with white, the color of light, and moving toward gold, a representation of full enlightenment. In the mythology of the people of Ecbatana, the divine was depicted by the circle of the heavens; the plan of their city created a microcosm of a holy macrocosm.

The original city of Baghdad, now subsumed by the growth of centuries, crowned more than 3,700 years of refinement of the circular city. Primal concepts of time and space guided its conception. A precise time—August 1, 762, under the sign of Leo—was selected for beginning construction on the site. A regional sense of place was gained by positioning the city in relation to the Euphrates River. Baghdad was enclosed by concentric brick walls measuring more than 4.5 miles in diameter. At the center stood the community mosque and the palace of the caliph. A residential area ringed the city just inside the outer wall. Four covered gateways divided this ring of houses into four equal quadrants, each quadrant containing twelve equal-sized neighborhoods. The four gates connected the city to the four gates of heaven, the four quarters of space. Movement toward the center of the city duplicated the movement of the human spirit toward the innermost realms of existence, the hidden treasure within the body, the kingdom of heaven within. The square plan of the mosque and palace at the city's center faced outward toward the all-encompassing circular walls—a movement that corresponded to the expansion of consciousness to embrace the totality of existence. Within this strict geometry, the expansion and contraction of collective consciousness flowed in endless cycles of renewal.

REGENERATION

Linking a city to land and climate plays an essential role in a community's sacredness. When cities in different parts of the globe appear the same, it is because their connection to the earth has been forgotten. Wind, rain, sun, hills, and valleys are suppressed in the mechanical architecture of uniformity. The urban landscape is cut off from the renewing power of the terrain and the restorative cycles of sun and moon.

When the city is connected to nature, the soul of community can be renewed. An extreme example of this took place in ancient Egypt. Every year communities along the Nile would be washed away when the river flooded its banks. After the waters had receded, the people would reestablish the boundaries of society. Year by year the measured areas of the village shifted, attuning human patterns of dwelling to the varying patterns of the earth. If the planetary and stellar configurations had also changed, the temple astronomer might suggest a new location and orientation for the community's sacred center.

In India, the city of Benares gains spiritual sustenance from its relationship to the sacred Ganges River. During the Holi festival in the spring the children and spirited adults playfully dash through the streets squirting each other with colored dyes. At sunset the entire community gathers at the river to wash off the dye and symbolically purify the body of the city. Every citizen, even the poorest beggar, dons new clothes to reflect nature's new growth in spring.

Attuning the city to the forces of nature encourages people to consistently renew their collective dwelling place by reenacting the genesis of community. Festivals and ceremonies repeat the sacred event that gave birth to ordered city life. In Babylon, this took the form of the *akitu* ceremony, which was performed during the last days of the passing year and the first days of the new one. The ritual involved solemnly reciting the *Poem of Creation*, which described the combat between the hero Marduk and the ocean monster Tiamat. Two groups of actors relived the mythic battle by playing out the moment that Marduk put an end to chaos by defeating Tiamat. The hero then built the universe from pieces of the monster's body and created humankind from the blood of the demon Kingu. The end of the old year was a time when fires were extinguished, social confusion reigned, and excessive indulgence of every sort symbolized the retrogression of the world into chaos. The universe was thought to mythi-

The gods always play where groves are near, rivers, mountains, and springs, and in towns with pleasure gardens.
Brihat Samhita

Everyone has got to sit down and give [his] heart a chance to unfold and let the things that are deepest in [him] come up and speak to [him].
Alfred A. Montapert

cally descend into the primordial waters on the final day of the year. For a time, Tiamat, the monster of darkness, formlessness, and anarchy, held the upper hand. But Marduk fought back and order was restored. By partaking of the dissolution and re-creation of the cosmos, the community touched the sacred moment of universal genesis and was healed—attaining symbolic rebirth in a stronger, more vital form.

Urban architecture provides a wide range of settings to support the rituals of community renewal. It facilitates the rights of passage that link each individual to the wholeness of community. The baptistery cups the waters of purification where infants travel into a realm of wholeness. Teenagers come of age these days at the department of motor vehicles, where they must submit to a driving test before being entrusted with one of our culture's central power symbols, the automobile. Marriage has its wedding chapel, death its burial ground. Traditionally community rituals never tried to resist the cycles of nature; they prepared the society to endure the cold of winter, celebrated the renewal of spring, engaged in the planting of summer, and gave thanks for the harvest of fall.

The Greek architect . . . celebrated three deathless themes: the sanctity of the earth, the tragic stature of mortal life on earth, and the whole natures of those recognitions of the facts of existence, which are the gods.
Vincent Scully

Western approach of Acropolis.

178

In ancient Greece the Panathenaic Festival intimately linked architecture to the ritual renewal of Athens. Before dawn the citizens gathered outside the city among the tombs of the prominent dead. Just after sunrise the entire population reentered the outer gate and proceeded along the wide street that led directly to the marketplace. A group of maidens headed the procession, carrying a ritual tunic they had woven during the year. The monumental garment was decorated with scenes from the battle of the gods and the giants. At the prearranged signal, the tunic was raised onto a cart designed to look like a ship and tied to the mast, like a sail. The maidens remained at the head of the line, followed by the cavalry and charioteers, the elders bearing olive branches (the tree of the goddess Athena), musicians playing sacred songs, young men carrying jugs of oil and wine, and shepherds herding the sacrificial sheep and heifers. The procession traveled through the marketplace and then began its steep climb toward the Acropolis, circling the hill and stopping at the foot of the western slope. The enormous tunic was untied and given to the maidens to carry up the towering steps.

If the measurement of the Temple is in every way perfect, there will be perfection in the universe as well.
Mayamata

Propylaia, looking toward the Parthenon.

179

Western facade of the Parthenon.

As they made their ascent the citizens could see to their left the outline of the temple to Athena Nike. Its elegant design perfectly symbolized Victory, the lady who was often portrayed in painting and sculpture touching down from above in a hesitant flurry. The exaggerated column capitals at the corners were meant to lead the eye toward the site of the heroic sea battle that liberated Athens and the rest of mainland Greece.

The procession continued through the Propylaia, a small building that served as a gateway to the Acropolis and provided entry to the adjacent temple. During the year it acted as a lavishly decorated refreshment stop for pilgrims. Its intimate scale constricted the sense of space and focused attention on the Parthenon beyond.

The procession with the maidens and their enormous tunic then traveled across the rock floor that sloped upward from the gate to the Parthenon and ascended the monumental steps at the west facade. From here they could see the outline of the pediment, with its sculptural depiction of Athena and Poseidon surrounded by other gods battling over the rulership of Attica. On the band that ran along the north side of the temple, facing the direction of Troy, Lapiths and Centaurs, Greeks and Amazons, Greeks and Trojans wrestled; on the southern band, giants and gods were locked in titanic combat. Rather than extolling the victory of one side or the other, the din of battle was portrayed. The Athenian spirit praised timeless idealism, but it also glorified the heroic plunge into the thick and thin of living.

A band of carvings running the length of the building depicted the citizens themselves high on the temple wall. It showed the same procession that had brought the citizens to this point. The architecture portrayed the relationship between the goddess, the citizens, and the physical structure of the city.

Traveling around the temple, the citizens could see the birth of Athena chiseled into the eastern pediment, the goddess emanating in full bloom from Zeus' brow. The maidens handed the ritual tunic to the priests, who, in turn, carried it into the shrine. Looking through the towering eastern doorway, they could catch a glimpse of Athena's form at the end of the great central hall. Two rows of monumental pillars framed the imposing gold-and-ivory statue of the warrior goddess who held a spear in one hand and shield in the other.

Statue of Athena Parthenos (reconstruction view), Parthenon.

Erechtheion, Caryatid Porch.

*Sooner or later cities will
express the highest
spiritual life and power
that they are capable of.*
Bernard Maybeck

The crowd then moved toward the Erechtheion, an elegantly designed temple to Athena, whose warm, refined, domestic details acted as a counterpoint to the masculine sternness of the Parthenon. This structure sheltered the trident mark of Poseidon, who drew salt water from a rock during a battle with Athena. The goddess fought back by spearing the rock and producing an olive tree that is still growing on the spot. In the plaza between the two temples, the diverse manifestations of the goddess Athena could be seen.

Today stadiums seem to be the city's gathering places for re-generating community—settings where the solitude of personal training enters the public arena of competitive event. The essence of athletics, interestingly enough, is found in the Greek word *athlos*, meaning "contest." When a citizen of ancient Greece won an Olympic contest, the city would tear down part of its walled fortifications as a symbolic act—showing the world that the place that had fostered such a hero was not afraid of foreign invasion. In this way the early Olympic games gave individual athletes the opportunity to bring together disparate communities into a fellowship of sacredness.

To build a temple or a city is equivalent to reiterating the construction of the Universe.
Mircea Eliade

Baltimore's Camden Yards by HOK Sports Facilities Group is integrated into the city's fabric, using baseball's popularity as a hub of community renewal. U.S. Representative David Bonior of Michigan says that "the history of ballparks is American history in its purest form. . . . They are truly shrines that future generations have a right to inherit."

NEW PATTERNS OF UNITY

In recent times festivals of renewal have lost their power to heal the city's wounds. Mass celebrations seem out of touch with present needs. The collective soul calls for more individualized pathways that link each person to a greater sense of wholeness.

The work of performance artist Mierle Laderman Ukeles offers an example of how one person can begin to heal the city's soul. Since 1978 she has been artist-in-residence at the New York City Department of Sanitation. Twenty-six thousand tons of garbage are generated in New York City every day. If the sanitation workers didn't do their jobs, the city would drown in its own waste. In 1980 and 1981 Ukeles performed an artwork called *Touch Sanitation* by walking eight hours a day through the city's five boroughs, personally shaking hands with each of the 8,500 people in the department. After attending roll call with the sanitation workers, she would walk their routes with them, video camera in hand. Along the way Ukeles performed a ritual in which she faced each person, shook his or her hand, and said, "Thank you for keeping New York alive." The artist's hope is that her handshakes "will eventually burn an image into the public's mind that every time they throw something out, human hands have to take it away." She feels that this work "is about healing bad feelings and the workers' sense of isolation. Many of them said, 'I never believed anything like this would ever happen.'"

In the process of shaking hands with the sanitation workers, Ukeles was told about the offensive names people call them. Taunts of "dirtbag, can man, slimeball, slob, and trash hound" are yelled by the very people the workers are trying to serve. Ukeles found that the workers felt that people saw them as part of the garbage. One day the crew needed a breather and rested on the stoop of a nearby house. A woman opened her window and screamed, "Get away from me, you smelly garbage men! I don't want you stinking up my steps." The worker said, "For seventeen years that has stuck in my throat. Today, you cleared it away."

This experience led Ukeles to create a ritual called *Cleaning the Bad Names*. The artist duplicated two sanitation environments. One facility imitated an old district office, which was furnished with objects recovered from the garbage. The other room was modern and sterile, housing only a computer and a Nautilus weight-training machine. On the windows of the gallery Ukeles wrote the insulting

Wanting to reform the world without discovering one's true self is like trying to cover the whole world with leather to avoid the pain of walking on stones and thorns. It is much simpler to wear shoes.
Ramana Maharishi

names that people call the workers. At the opening of the exhibit, she handed sponges to the gathering of sanitation workers, art commissioners, artists, city officials, and company presidents, inviting them to wash the offensive names away.

For her next project, called *Flow City,* Ukeles plans to build an observation deck to allow the public to view thousands of tons of garbage leaving the city, making the transition from trucks onto barges for the journey to the Staten Island landfill. Here the citizens of New York will be able to traverse a ramp made of recycled materials to reach a glass viewing platform where they can watch the dumping operations, gain information about ecosystems and waste management from a bank of video monitors, and view the Hudson River.

Through insight and an expanded sense of self we can begin to soften and reshape the rigid boundaries of the city into forms that respond to the fluid reality of our minds and bodies. Just as every building is born as a vision in someone's mind, every city is the child of a community's collective dream. The hopes and fears of the shared mind flow into the architectural body that supports a society's modes of seeing the world.

Here and there groups and individuals are reshaping community environments to reflect new patterns of wholeness. In the Pacific Northwest, thirty families live in a five-acre pedestrian village on Bainbridge Island. A group of small homes clustered around a common dining hall, child-care center, and recreation area are organized to reflect the ideals of the Winslow CoHousing Group. Developed in Scandinavia, CoHousing synthesizes the privacy and equity of home ownership with the companionship and efficiency of community. Doors are seldom locked, cooking duties are shared, and everyone spends time cultivating the communal garden. Residents gather for meals in the central dining hall five nights a week and for brunch on Sundays. All the citizens participate in child care, with retired people acting as part-time grandparents.

The architectural and planning team of Andres Duany and Elizabeth Plater-Zyberk has drawn on the principles used to create the balanced, human scale found in eighteenth-century American towns and applied them to the design of modern communities. In minitowns, such as Seaside and Windsor, they have developed zoning and design codes that organize public buildings, streets, and homes in

Where we live is the Buddha's realm, the world of the gods. Paradise is where we live, so we keep it clean and beautiful. That is why we tend our gardens so carefully and treat them with such artistry.
Sobin Yamada

A house is imagined as a concentrated being. It appeals to our consciousness of centrality.
Gaston Bachelard

patterns that foster natural social interaction while respecting individual privacy. The planning guidelines encourage architects to broaden their awareness by integrating the design of each building into the wholeness of the urban fabric.

In the Brazilian city of Curitiba, an ambitious program to revitalize urban life has met with great success. In 1970, Mayor Jaime Lerner initiated low-cost programs to build parks, control garbage, house the poor, and develop a mass-transit system. When the work began, Curitiba had only five square feet of open space per person; now it provides 550 square feet, even though the population has increased 164 percent. "Services like parks and high-quality public transportation give dignity to the citizen," says Lerner, "and if people feel respected, they will assume responsibility to solve other problems." Based on this growing consciousness, forty centers for feeding and educating street children have been established. The recycling of garbage is almost a religion. In the city's many parks, jogging paths are lit with lamps made from soda bottles. Curitiba's environmental department was constructed with reclaimed telephone poles. Former squatters, outside the city's sanitation pickup routes, take their own garbage to designated locations in exchange for bags of vegetables. Neighborhoods that used to be carpeted with trash and plagued by disease are now free of litter, and the people are much healthier.

A far-reaching vision for urban renewal has been proposed by a modern-day seer. Drawing on the ancient Indian knowledge of building in accord with natural law called Maharishi Sthapatya-Veda, Maharishi Mahesh Yogi, founder of Transcendental Meditation, has proposed a program for creating cities and towns that promote health and balance in mind, body, and surroundings. Sthapatya-Veda provides a method of architecture and community design that focuses on establishing individuals and society in relation to the environment for the purpose of gaining "full support of the evolutionary power of natural law in daily life." The plan calls for ringing existing cities with a series of small towns that nurture health and well-being. Each community will consist of at least one to two hundred homes and public amenities based on the following principles: low-density housing to offset the buildup of stress and crime that results from crowded and stifling living conditions; nontoxic construction and use of natural building materials to counteract sick-building syndrome (which results from the outgassing of toxic chemicals commonly

Every corner in a house . . . is a symbol of solitude for the imagination.
Gaston Bachelard

You examine a historic form and see whether the effect it produces on your mind matches the feeling you are trying to portray.
Bernard Maybeck

The house allows one to dream in peace.
Gaston Bachelard

found in modern construction materials); energy-efficient construction, using "thick-walled" construction and solar energy to provide shelter without relying on mechanical means of heating and cooling; generous green space, weaving gardens, tree-lined streets, bodies of water, and wooded areas into the fabric of community to balance stressful influences, provide adequate fresh air, and make nature a part of the community; nonpolluting vehicles such as electric automobiles to decrease noise and air pollution; community farms to provide natural, locally grown, organic food; and in-home telecommunications to reduce or eliminate commuting and allow individuals to work and shop from their homes. The town centers of these communities call for amenities that enrich body, mind, and spirit: an Ayurvedic health center, to restore balance in mind and body through a five-thousand-year-old system of natural medicine; a school whose curriculum includes the traditional disciplines of mathematics, literature, science, and art in relation to the inner development of the students' own consciousness; and a festival hall for cultural and social activities.

At Seaside, Florida, designed by Andres Duany and Elizabeth Plater-Zyberk, a walkway lined by picket fences helps to create a humane, livable community.

"Build a city and bring the universe to it," suggested King Dur-yodhona to his son in the epic *Mahabharata*. Since the earliest times, towns and villages have been built in imitation of cosmic patterns of existence. The decay and destruction of a community was seen as a descent into chaos. Any victory over the forces of this decay re-produced the paradigmatic victory of the gods over anarchy. For-tifications, trenches, labyrinths, and ramparts were often used as a community's magical defenses, for they were designed more to repel invasion by demons than attacks by human beings. In northern In-dia, during epidemics, a circle was often drawn around the village to keep the demons of sickness from entering.

Through modern technology and communications, the aware-ness of the city has expanded to encompass the globe. Our hearts and minds are often more deeply affected by political strife, violence, and famine in Beijing, Jerusalem, or Moscow than by the conflicts in our own neighborhood. Ecological consciousness has dissolved the boun-daries that once blinded us to the connections between one city and another; the pollution from a Pittsburgh steel mill creates the acid rain that falls on Boston. The boundaries of a traditional Japanese vil-lage were defined by the distance that the sound of a drum could carry. Anyone within earshot of the sound was considered part of the village. Following this tradition, a member of a contemporary Jap-anese troupe of drummers, the Kodo Players, which performs in countries around the globe, said that he considers all those who hear their concerts as parts of their village.

In this light, the global city needs no protection from outer forces. Any decay begins inside the collective body. It appears that urban renewal can only take place when the consciousness of its cit-izens turns back on itself, regenerating the city from within. The es-sential task is to heal the soul of community through compassion for its mind and body—people shaping its mind, while buildings and streets form its body. Because the technological architecture of the modern city promotes fragmentation and conflict in collective con-sciousness, wholeness must be brought to it. For the urban environ-ment to be revived, it must be cared for, as a kind doctor would care for a patient—not with fear and dread, but with friendship and love. A felt connection to the physical and spiritual world can then be re-stored, making whole the gathering of humanity.

There are gods of the house, and our daily work is a way of acknowledging these home spirits that are important in sustaining our lives. To them, a scrub brush is a sacramental object, and when we use this implement with care we are giving something to the soul. In this sense, cleaning a bathroom is a form of therapy because there is a correspondence between the actual room and a chamber of the heart.
Thomas Moore

Seeing and Creating

1. As you move through your community, become aware of how the various districts, buildings, streets, and public spaces express different inflections of collective consciousness. In what ways does the architecture of a school differ from that of a city hall, the performing arts center, or a hospital? Perceive the underlying forces that shape the physical forms of these institutions, such as culture, economics, and climate. See each of these places as a conscious entity that has a distinct personality. Imagine what these different architectural citizens might say to you if you sat down to talk with them. How did they come to be here? What are the problems they face? What will heal them?

2. Notice the components of the sacred that give form to the architectural bodies of these places: gate, path, and lotus seat, steeple and sanctuary, the eight archetypes of building form, the body's form and function, and the influences of sunlight. How might these be redesigned or altered to bring greater wholeness and creativity to the city?

3. Feel the connection between your own consciousness and the aspect of collective consciousness that has shaped each place. What facet of yourself Is expressed in the post office, courthouse, office building, restaurant, etc.? Do you see qualities such as communication, justice, compassion, competition, service, enjoyment? What other characteristics of consciousness can you perceive?

4. Imagine how each of these places might be used as a setting for community ceremonies and festivals that could revitalize the city. How could they be altered to support seasonal celebration?

5. If you own or manage a store or business, perceive its relationship to the rest of the city and envision ways that you might decorate or remodel it to enhance the community. Think of the role your business plays in the context of the whole, and how its design might strengthen that role.

NINE

A Sacred World

Inside this clay jar there are canyons and pine mountains,
and the maker of canyons and pine mountains!
All seven oceans are inside, and hundreds and millions of stars.
The acid that tests gold is there, and the one who judges jewels.
And the music from the strings that no one touches,
and the source of all water.
If you want the truth, I will tell you the truth:
Friend, listen: the God whom I love is inside.

KABIR

Our perception of the sacred can either be limited or liberated by architecture. Seeing a pillar only as a physical structure, we restrict our ability to experience the sacredness within it. Defining the Washington Monument, for example, only by its date of construction, architect, cost, height, and stonework freezes it in a rigid materialism. Calling the memorial a symbol of America's aspirations expands the definition into the realm of consciousness, but restricts it to the hopes of one nation. Seeing it as an axial pillar, a universal archetype of psychological stability at the center of a revolving world, opens our awareness to greater possibilities. Transcending even this definition and beholding the monument not as a symbol of this or that idea, but as a direct manifestation of the sacred, liberates our minds from the isolating influence of physical form, uniting the life of the monument with the core of our being.

*There is religion
in everything around us.*
John Ruskin

*To the enlightened brahmin all
the Vedas are of no more use
than is a small well in
a place flooded with water
on every side.*
Bhagavad Gita

*I think that's the essence of
craftsmanship. That the
trivial is transparent.
It's transparent to the eternal.
And the eternal is
embodied in the trivial, in the
here and now.*
Arthur Koestler

The same idea is suggested in Buddhist philosophy by the saying "Kill the Buddha." A shocking statement perhaps, but one that cuts to the quick. All symbols, even those as expansive as a temple, church, or synagogue, are made of boundaries that can limit our thoughts, words, and actions. In architectural terms, the commandment "Thou shalt have no other gods before me" suggests that only by seeing through the outer appearance of these supreme symbols— those that embody the ultimate mental constructs—can we experience the most awakened states of heart and mind, attaining more joy and freedom in life.

This book has discussed how elemental forms of architecture relate to particular qualities of consciousness, how a doorway, for instance, expresses the idea of transition. The sacred can be found within a door, but it is not the door itself. Sacredness is within the portal, central aisle, and altar of a church, but it is not bound by these things. Peace, inspiration, and renewal make a shrine holy, not the stone and glass of its walls. Subtler and more elusive than any material structure, sacredness is a living presence that surrounds and permeates visible forms.

Paradoxically, without a physical structure the sacred cannot be perceived. Just as space is made useful by surrounding it with walls and a roof, the sacred becomes perceptible by defining it with building form. The columns that border the nave of a church, the ceiling that soars heavenward, and the altar that supports the mass reveal a boundless reality. The elements of architecture provide finite windows of form that frame a formless, infinite realm.

Sacredness is not confined to religious buildings. Even though transcendent realities seem more apparent in the precinct of a temple than in the central aisle of a shopping mall, the sacred resides within both environments. The ability to discern this subtle realm in any setting depends on understanding five layers of perception: the glittering mask, the silent core, symbols of totality, the garden of infinite correlation, and the house of the self.

THE GLITTERING MASK

"The world is a cluttered house that hides the holy one," was the wise teaching of an ancient sage. Architecture veils the silent spirit behind facades of steel and glass. Its forms, colors, and textures attract our awareness to the surface of life rather than to its depths. The numerous facets of a building's exterior shatter the unified light of the sacred into countless, fragmented rays. Dazzled by these isolated bits of creation, wholeness goes unnoticed. According to Mircea Eliade, "The great paradox common to all religions is that God in showing himself to mankind is free to take any form, but by asserting this freedom he limits himself and reduces himself to a fragment of the wholeness he represents."

Architecture's glittering mask is fabricated from an ever-shifting scenery of sensory experience. Footsteps echo down the hall, sunlight sweeps along a colonnade, the texture of an oak handrail accompanies us up a flight of steps. Each of these sensations shimmers across the quiet expanse of the sacred. Discerning the transparency of this sparkling disguise is a necessary step toward perceiving the spiritual essence of life.

Masks are translucent, because they simultaneously hide and reveal the identities of those who wear them. War masks, fertility masks, and initiation masks are tools for unearthing latent strengths and abilities within the psyche. Eskimos believe that the wearer is imbued with the soul represented by the mask; to don the mask representing a totem is to become that totem. A mask can announce the manifestation of a mythological figure or represent ancestors; it stirs the memory of primordial wholeness and legendary deeds. An actor who takes on the costume of Abraham Lincoln brings to life a set of cultural recollections, recalling the attempt to heal and unify a divided and chaotic nation.

In a similar vein, architects who use devices such as Roman temple fronts at the entrances to banks, libraries, state capitols, and other monumental buildings employ building masks that draw on the mythic images of "the grandeur that was Rome." The simple gabled roof and pillars of the temple front also evoke primal elements of construction, the most fundamental of architectural shelters. Different architectural styles present diverse masks of consciousness. The Tudor style, for instance, can express the spirit of a simpler, less mechanistic time. An abode of glass and steel offers a glossy cover for the energy and information culture of modern life. These and other styles present rigid architectural forms that veil the flow of consciousness, the flashing eyes and sculptured mouth that reveal the play of human life behind the stiff disguise.

O God, in every temple I see people that see thee. And in every language I hear them praise thee. If it be a mosque, people murmur the Holy Prayer. And if it be a Christian church, the bell is rung in love of thee. Sometimes I frequent the Christian cloister and sometimes the mosque. But it is thou whom I seek from temple to temple.
Abul-Fazl

Don't be confused by surfaces; in the depths everything becomes law.
Rainer Maria Rilke

Architectural devices such as the templelike front of the New York Stock Exchange draw on mythic images of the past, giving the building the aura of timelessness, stability, and refined culture.

Perceiving the Glittering Mask

■ Stand in front of your house or another building. Notice the elements that make up its facade: walls, pillars, doors and windows, ornament, etc. Look at the play of light on these components; see their various colors. Listen to the sounds of traffic, people, birds, wind, and so on that bounce off the facade. Touch the textures and shapes of the different materials and elements.

■ Perceive the facade of this building not as a collection of physical objects but as a glittering mask of sights, sounds, textures, and shapes.

■ Imagine the builders who constructed this facade and the consciousness that flowed through their minds and bodies into the architecture. Imagine the person who hired them. Think of the specific requirements that he or she communicated to the builders, such as the number of bedrooms, the relationship of the living room to the dining room and kitchen, or feelings the guests might experience as they approached the building.

■ Think of the vision that motivated the owner to erect this building. Now go beyond this vision and experience the field of consciousness that gave rise to the thoughts and actions that led to its construction.

■ Stand back from the building and remember the layers of the facade that you just experienced: physical, sensory, mental, emotional, and the field of consciousness behind all of these layers.

■ Choose another building and go through the process described above. See how a building with a different outer appearance masks the qualities of consciousness of those who built it and dwell within it.

■ Find a temple, synagogue, church, or other sacred building that embodies your spiritual beliefs. See how its design puts those beliefs into physical form. Relate these forms to the fundamental architectural patterns discussed in this book: gate, path, and lotus seat, steeple and sanctuary, floor, walls, pillars, roof, space, doors and windows, ornament, and rooms. Perceive these architectural patterns as expressions of different qualities of thought and feeling such as transforming, searching, fulfilling, aspiring, healing,

The intrusions of the "mundane" become agents of the sublime.
Lynda Sexson

When you gaze at an object, you bring blessing to it. For through contemplation, you know that it is absolutely nothing without the divinity that permeates it. By means of this awareness, you draw greater vitality to that object from the divine source of life.
Dov Baer of Mezritch

supporting, sheltering, hoping, imagining, transcending, rejoicing, and integrating. See how specific beliefs and architectural forms are supported by universal qualities of thought and feeling and architectural patterns. Look beyond the boundaries of these glittering masks to perceive the underlying field of consciousness from which they arise.

All this talk and turmoil and noise and movement and desire is outside the veil; inside the veil is silence and calm and peace.
Abu Yazid al-Bistami

THE SILENT CORE

Buddha was once asked, "Are you a god?"
"No," he replied.
"Are you an angel?"
"No."
"Are you a saint?"
"No."
"What are you then?"
"I am awake."

Understanding architecture's glittering mask is only a means of discovering its inner life. In the above story, Buddha suggests that we look beyond the outer masks of name and form to see his true nature. Once past a building's outer mask, however, we reach what looks like a void. In reality, this silent core is an inexhaustible source of awakened consciousness, full of energy, intelligence, and bliss. Like the empty hub that allows the wheel to turn, or the hollow that makes a teacup useful, the boundless core of awareness gives form and meaning to architecture's boundaries. The Upanishads describe it as "That which makes the tongue speak but which cannot be spoken by the tongue . . . That which makes the mind think but which cannot be thought by the mind . . . That which makes the eye see but which cannot be seen by the eye . . . That which makes the ear hear but which cannot be heard by the ear . . ."

The silent core is an organizing principle that shapes disparate building elements into environments of totality. It establishes a dimensionless, timeless locus at the hub of diverse shapes and experiences. The center, being a place of crossing and turning, becomes the ultimate reference point in the geography of consciousness. Holy cities such as Jerusalem, Rome, and Mecca are each seen as occupying the center of the sacred world. The centers of medieval maps are marked by Jerusalem. Rome is the seat of the Catholic Church. Mecca is the psychological center of the Muslim cosmos.

In all of these circumstances, the center of the world is constructed by human hands. Women and men mold the earth into a reflection of totality, an architectural distillation of the universe. The builder's vision shapes the natural environment into a form that echoes the inner landscape of his or her consciousness. Because brick and wood can be assembled anywhere, the center of the world can be built anywhere, in a home, office building, or supermarket.

The glittering mask and the silent core are both essential to sacredness in architecture. The workings of the soul cannot be seen if there are no tangible structures to reflect its light. The physical boundaries of a building can lead the mind toward transcendent realities. The bricks of an arched window, for example, frame a view of the boundless sky. Form and formlessness, movement and stillness together constitute the sacred wholeness of architecture. Every act of construction is the marriage of outer structure to silent core. Wood, brick, metal, and glass are molded to the consciousness of those who dwell inside. Notice how the outer appearance of homes and businesses reflects the personalities of their inhabitants. By seeing the union of architecture's outer mask and its silent essence, every structure can become a practical symbol of totality.

The sounds of the streams splash out the Buddha's sermon. Don't say that the deepest meaning comes only from one's mouth. Day and night 80,000 poems arise one after the other and not a single word has been spoken.
Anonymous

Entering the Silent Core

- Visit a building with a large interior space such as the lobby of a hotel, the atrium of an office building, an airport, or a shopping mall.

- See how the floor, walls, and room define the space. Notice how the other rooms of the building are related to this core.

- Watch people moving through it. See the play of light and color. Listen to the voices, footsteps, elevator bells, and other sounds that pass through the core.

- Look at the spaces between people and objects in this place. Listen to the silence between words, footsteps, and other sounds. Experience how the silent core organizes the life of this building.

197

SYMBOLS OF TOTALITY

The symbolic power of sacred buildings cannot be exhausted. Holy shrines receive endless streams of pilgrims because they establish places where mind/body wholeness is consistently regained. Common settings can also provide access to continuous regeneration. Day after day we are renewed by the rest and dreamtime of the bedroom, waters of the bath, and nourishment of the kitchen. Office buildings and schools, despite their pressures and conflicts, provide settings to gain insight, spark creativity, and enjoy friends.

These structures of totality embody multiple layers of meaning. A Native American tepee, for example, is at once a house, a ceremonial structure, a depiction of the cosmic mountain, and a diagram of the human spirit's journey from earthly diversity to heavenly unity. Louis Kahn described how the simple design of a chapel offers more than one level of experience. He said that it provides "a sanctuary for those who want to kneel. Around the sanctuary is an ambulatory . . . for those who are not sure, but want to be near. Outside is a court for those who want to feel the presence of the chapel. And the court has a wall. Those who pass the wall can wink at it."

We cannot, however, experience wholeness in architecture by understanding how its various pieces are put together. During the construction of the houses I design, my clients tend to focus on the smallest details: the shape of a countertop edge, placement of an electrical receptacle, or color of a cabinet knob. Only after moving in and allowing the parts to fade from their minds do they gain an appreciation of the home's totality. The process of dwelling in the house begins to fill their awareness. Eating, sleeping, bathing, and other activities integrate building elements and furniture into a living symbol of wholeness.

The process of dwelling can provide direct experience of the transcendent forces shaping a building. A bathtub, for example, can be perceived as a metaphor for purification and revitalization, transforming clumps of porcelain and pipe into emblems of the sacred. From this perspective, the solidity of architecture is dissolved, revealing dimensions of the soul that are beyond ordinary sensory experience. The unique conditions of this or that window are surpassed, disclosing universal archetypes of the consciousness dwelling within each building element. Each distinct shape is magnified by the ocean of energy and intelligence within it.

Take, for example, a pencil, ashtray, anything, and holding it before you in both hands, regard it for a while. Forgetting its use and name, yet continuing to regard it, ask yourself seriously, "What is it?" . . . Its dimension of wonder opens; for the mystery of the being of that thing is identical with the mystery of the being of the universe— and yourself.
Joseph Campbell

To perceive architecture in this manner is to encounter the sacred at every point in the environment. Since 99 percent of our lives takes place within some type of building, street, or designed landscape, any moment offers an opening to the inexhaustible powers of the soul. Each setting of symbolic elements reveals another layer of reality that was unformed and elusive in neighboring contexts. The doorway to a house reflects a different nuance of energy and intelligence than the doorway to a bank or a post office. Every stage of encounter discloses another inflection of consciousness. Passing through one plane of awareness after the other, we enter deeper and deeper strata of existence. We come to dwell in a domain of sacredness.

Life to us
is a symbol to be lived.
Lame Deer

Borobudur, aerial view.

The mountainous Buddhist stupa of Borobudur in Java presents a clear example of symbolic architectural form. This monumental work depicts an architectural body of awakened consciousness and serves as a vehicle for carrying human life to a plane of awareness where enlightenment can be "touched." The stupa is designed to duplicate the transformation of consciousness one experiences in meditation and during the path to enlightenment. It brings the archetypal journey of heart and mind to the obvious level of physical form.

Approaching Borobudur, we encounter a mystery; we cannot see its totality. The stupa—the symbolic body of the Buddha—looms

Whatever a symbol tries to show us, it is . . . the unity between different levels of the real.
Mircea Eliade

He made these His works manifest, to the end that the intelligent might contemplate them; and He brought into view all that was in His invisible world, that the observant might behold it and acknowledge His Skill and Peerlessness and Omnipotence and Soleness, and not stand in need of proof and demonstration.
Ikhwan al-Safa

above us like a multistoried fortress. Entering the temple we penetrate the anatomy of the "Awakened One." Moving through the galleries, we discern nothing but statues in niches and bas-reliefs adorning the walls. The different planes of experience unfold step by step, a sequential flowering. By absorbing each scene, one after the other, through the mile and a half of galleries, we gradually awaken to expanded levels of consciousness. The physical task of slowly ascending this sacred mountain allows the steps of transformation to saturate mind and body. On the physical level we reenact the soul's journey to liberation. Passing through the galleries and opening our awareness to the sculptural messages, we gradually realize the degrees of expanded reality, the shades of meditation phrased in stone. Reaching the pinnacle of the stupa, we can look back at all the stages that led us to this point. A vision of totality is attained; we can see how each small piece of the stupa is glorified by working in conjunction with every other piece. We behold a symbol of the universe in its primal condition, a united diversity.

The stupa represents a self-sufficient microcosm of the world. Each step through it awakens the primordial memory of our true nature—the recollection of the totality of existence within our own awareness. Borobudur is an architectural image of a living body that harmonizes the needs of its various organs and limbs without suppressing their diversity. It is a vision of the ultimate expansion of human consciousness. The stupa silently whispers that spiritual regeneration is not gained by leaving the world, but by expanding our awareness to embrace the all.

Even though wholeness is usually hidden beneath the fragmented surfaces of industrial society, we can find the sacred by looking deeply into common circumstances. On its face, a drive-through bank has little in common with Borobudur. But as we wait among the lines of automobiles for our turn at the teller, similarities arise. Each vehicle's curving roof, sides, and openings form a sleek architectural niche for the passengers within. Lined up beside us, they frame the gradations of human consciousness: anxiety, boredom, peace, bemusement, liberation (for those who have passed through the teller's window), and other emotions. The taillights of the car in front slow our progress and recall the twin pillars of Borobudur's gateways, the duality of anticipation and frustration that must be passed to reach the teller. While we inch forward, the circles of the steering wheel

Borobudur, ground-level view of the exterior.

and tires recall the universal symbol of wholeness and the eternal cycles of creation, dissolution, and renewal. Stage by stage, each person progresses toward the teller, the deity of abundance enshrined in a glistening cube of bulletproof glass. Paying homage with a prescribed formula (a deposit or withdrawal slip), we attain fulfillment (albeit momentary).

Symbols of totality can be found within supermarkets, gas stations, office buildings, and other common settings. Seeing through our limited notions of these places, architecture becomes porous to the radiance of the sacred. When ordinary buildings are perceived as emblems of wholeness, our immediate reality glows with the light of consciousness. Everyday life is not limited; no object or action is isolated. What seemed like a chaotic environment is discerned as a harmonious system of integration and assimilation. Buildings are transformed from solid objects into gateways through which the soul can manifest itself. Gaining a sacred perspective on the places in which we dwell translates our human condition into cosmic terms. It reveals the interdependence between actions within each part of the environment and its totality. By connecting human architecture to universal design, isolation is dissolved. The vastness of the cosmos becomes as familiar as our own house. Individual, subjective experience comes to share a universal perspective.

The elements of all things, whatever their mode, observe an inner order. It is this form that makes the universe resemble God.
Dante

201

Borobudur, galleries.

Borobudur, view from the top of the stupa.

EXPERIENCING
SYMBOLS OF TOTALITY

- Walk slowly through the different rooms in your house. Witness the thoughts and feelings that rise within you. Think of the qualities of consciousness that each room symbolizes. The kitchen could signify transformation (changing raw foodstuffs into a meal) and/or loving-kindness (the care of preparation). The dining room might connote desire (hunger) and/or fulfillment

- Become aware of the significance that different objects, furniture, utensils, pictures, etc. have for you. Graciousness might be embodied in a vase, tiredness in an old chair, incisiveness in a knife, or dreaminess in a painting.

- See how changes in the time of day alter the meaning you associate with the rooms and furnishings.

- After going through all the rooms, remember the different inflections of consciousness that you experienced. See if they express the full range of your personality. If there are qualities of awareness that you possess that you did not find, look again to see if you can locate them.

- Look beyond the specific characteristics of consciousness expressed in your house and perceive the field of awareness that gives rise to them.

- Stand outside your house and perceive it as a container of this entire spectrum of consciousness, a symbol of totality.

- Repeat the steps outlined above in relation to your town or city. Think of the different neighborhoods as rooms in the community's house.

When we investigate the invisible mechanics of nature, we find that everything in the universe is directly connected with everything else. Everything is constantly being influenced by everything else. No wave of the ocean is independent of any other.
Maharishi Mahesh Yogi

In my hands I hold a bowl of tea. I see all of nature represented in its green color. Closing my eyes I find green mountains and pure water within my own heart. I feel these become part of me.
Anonymous

THE GARDEN
OF INFINITE CORRELATION

Another way that architecture becomes a practical symbol of totality is through its relationship to the processes of nature. The ecosystem that ceaselessly creates, sustains, and renews life on earth is the preeminent example of wholeness; it presents an object lesson in the infinite correlation of countless individual lives. Architecture also offers us an example of the workings of nature. A roof must know the ways of rain and snow, a wall the traits of gravity and wind, a window the particulars of light and air.

Just because a building utilizes the laws of nature, however, does not mean that it is in harmony with ecological processes. A glance at any major city is proof enough that the way we build is out of sync with the way nature lives. The basic problem is that the fragmented viewpoint of industrial culture only uses limited aspects of nature's functioning. The old saying that a little knowledge is a dangerous thing is validated by the fact that we are the only species that fouls its own nest so thoroughly and dangerously.

Our industrial, materialistic view of architecture and nature is fragmented because we try to freeze the fluid actions of the environment in discrete frames. We attempt to stop the stream of living. Buildings routinely ignore the constant fluctuations in climate that surround them. They maintain constant levels of temperature and illumination by using polluting systems for heating, cooling, and lighting. Cut off from the local nuances of weather and terrain, this approach separates human life from the harmonious processes of nature. We are like the fish described by Dogen Kigen, the thirteenth-century Japanese philosopher: "Now when fish see water as a palace, it is just like human beings seeing a palace. They do not think it flows. If an outsider tells them, 'What you see as a palace is running water,' the fish will be astonished."

The entire universe is concentrated in a garden.
Sobin Yamada

Earth, sky, and human life are in constant flux. Architecture's true nature is found in the shimmering lake of consciousness.

To overcome the frozen, lifeless condition of industrial culture and dwell in sacred wholeness, we must attune architecture to nature's functioning. A detailed discussion of building in this way is beyond the scope of this book, but the essential point is that we begin to discover ways of creating dwellings that reflect the organic continuum of the earth's ecological systems. It is to shape architecture from a perspective that sees the rhythm of a building's structural elements as expressing an inner circulation of energy and information. Such a view does not consider architectural gestures, such as doors or roofs, as isolated from one another, nature, the human body, or the mind. Every building becomes a means of reconnecting to the flow of consciousness in nature and ourselves.

Within this approach, architecture's purpose is to provide a holistic experience of mind, body, and environment, one that takes priority over its stylistic image. This is not achieved by copying the external forms of leaves, rocks, and animals, but by imitating the internal patterns of energy and intelligence that create and sustain them. Instead of trying to reproduce nature's outer mask, we can create in a way that parallels natural processes. By following the organic impulse, the thirst for life and growth within ourselves, we can discover the endless universal play of new forms and relationships. To be organic, a pillar, for example, does not have to imitate the form of a plant or animal. Instead, it can copy the unseen forces that give an upward thrust to trees, cornstalks, and every other living thing that bursts through the soil toward the sun. A window does not look like an eye, but it duplicates the structures in nature that allow fish, eagles, frogs, and people to perceive light. Reproducing the gestures of nature by using the deeper powers that inform its outer look, we can produce architecture that reflects the wholeness of ecological systems—truly organic buildings.

Architecture designed from this standpoint is constructed on the inner life of the spirit. The work of architects and builders becomes connected to the flow of life. The physical environment is shaped according to qualities of sacredness, not quantities of matter. To express in buildings the deeper processes of nature, the mind must be attuned to natural law. The work itself then becomes a spiritual path. Designers and artisans who submit to the processes of nature and renounce ego-centered initiative give birth to buildings that serve as vehicles for guiding heart and mind to a comprehension of deeper

This dawning sense of the Within as reality when it is clearly seen as Nature will by way of glass make the garden be the building as much as the building will be the garden, the sky as treasured a feature of daily life as the ground itself.
Frank Lloyd Wright

If ever I have somehow come to realize God, if the vision of God has ever been granted to me, I must have received it through this world, through man, through trees and birds and beasts, the dust and soil.
Rabindranath Tagore

realities. They design in partnership with the intelligence that creates plants, animals, rivers, and solar systems. An architect or builder who looks to ecological systems for knowledge of design enters an apprenticeship to the cosmic architect, opening himself or herself to the secrets of creation. The Vedic builders, described in Chapter Six, shaped their buildings according to the specific site's relationship to the sun, not to the whims of fashion. The creators of Chartres, Rheims, and other Gothic cathedrals used geometric proportions found in nature to attune their work to universal design. A craftsperson who shapes a table in response to the grain of its oak planks extends the life of the tree into the activities of those who gather around it. Surrendering to the design of nature, we can build environments that are more harmonious, joyous, and free. Instead of producing a landscape of isolated, lifeless objects, we can create architecture that offers a series of potentialities to be realized, dwellings that reflect different planes of cosmic law.

You never enjoy the world aright till you see how sand exhibits the wisdom and power of God; and prize in everything the service which they do you by manifesting His glory and goodness to your soul.
Thomas Traherne

Connecting Architecture to Nature

■ Locate the various ways that the laws of nature are utilized in your house. See how the walls respond to gravity and deflect the wind, how the gutters and downspouts guide rainwater. Imagine how the foundation works with the soil to support the structure. Notice how water becomes steam on the stove and ice in the freezer. Look for other connections between natural processes and the place you live.

■ Think of the ways your house works to stop, or retard, the flow of nature. Notice how the heating and/or air-conditioning system counteracts the changes in outside air temperature, how electric lights maintain one level of illumination whether it is day or night, and how the water heater keeps the water warm. Look for other examples.

■ Find the ways that the architectural elements of your house express the gestures of nature. See the roof as an extension of falling water and the floor as the spreading earth. Discover the connections between the cone of a lampshade and a flame of fire, or the movement of curtains and the wind. Locate other ways that the gestures of nature are expressed in architecture.

■ Look at a tree. Notice how its design integrates the form and function of all its parts into a unified whole, how the leaves, branches, trunk, and roots work with each other for the health and beauty of the tree. Become aware of the ways in which the tree's design also responds to its surroundings—soil, rain, wind, sun, birds, other plants, etc. Perceive the intelligence that guides its growth and shape. See the design of your body in a similar way. Review Chapter Five to see how the intelligence that guides the form and function of your body is expressed in architecture. Try to locate the source of intelligence, the cosmic architect, that designs the tree and your body. Think of ways you could translate nature's architectural know-how into the design of your home.

THE HOUSE OF THE SELF

When we begin to experience architecture as so many layers of sacredness, buildings can become vehicles for transcending limited horizons and passing into realms of ever-expanding realization. Perceiving subtler and more far-reaching nuances of the connections between consciousness and the physical environment, we can cross threshold after threshold of understanding. Every design element from a doorknob to a city plaza then takes on the glow of a symbol that embodies our highest aspirations. Our awareness of the sacred dwelling within each architectural structure expands until we see every component as a reflection of life's totality. Finally our minds pierce the obscuring shroud of form to a realization that transcends form. We go beyond all symbols to direct cognitions of the source of every thing.

The gateway to this realization is not in some distant land. It is as close as the door to your own house. As Kabir says, "Are you looking for me? I am in the next seat. My shoulder is against yours. . . . When you really look for me, you will see me instantly—you will find me in the tiniest house of time." Discerning the sacred in every object and circumstance, we begin to live continuously in a consecrated world, a universe kept open by communication between all levels of existence. Human dwelling then partakes of sacred dwelling. Openings to the transcendent are perceived in every physical structure—from a windowsill to a galaxy. "Whoever can't see the whole in every part plays at blindman's buff; a wise man tastes the entire Tigris in every sip," was the wise observation of the eighteenth-century Indian poet Ghalib.

Art arises when the secret vision of the artist and the manifestation of nature agree to find new shapes.
Kahlil Gibran

He who sees Me everywhere, and sees everything in Me, I am not lost to him, nor is he lost to Me.
Bhagavad Gita

*A quick inventory back inside
the temple reveals that
the holy is made up of words
and works identical to all the
stuff of the profane world.*
Lynda Sexson

*A single atom of the sweetness
of wisdom in a man's
heart is better than a thousand
pavilions in Paradise.*
Abu Yazid al-Bistami

With the dawning of this awareness, distinctions between the profane and the sacred vanish. The word *profane* comes from Latin roots meaning "before the temple." When the temple's sacredness is seen in every part of a building or city, nothing is relegated to the profane steps before it. The sacred is no longer limited to religious settings; the entire world sparkles with vibrant consciousness. Age-old wounds caused by severing inner spirit from the houses and cities that shelter it are healed. Wholeness is restored not by escaping the boundaries of everyday living but by embracing them. The confines of walls and roofs become gateways to a more soulful life. Each thought and action in a spiritualized home or city becomes a sacred ritual. Every activity at work, school, or with the family offers a continuous connection to the inexhaustible source of existence.

But what about ugly, banal, or threatening environments, those that violate our standards of beauty, harmony, and order? Can the sacred be found in a garbage dump, oil refinery, or slum? These questions bring out a key understanding of the sacred. Sacredness transcends the dualities of living; it is too vast for the pairs of opposites to contain. Beauty is opposed by ugliness. Between these two extremes flows the sacred river of life. Despite its ugliness, a garbage dump provides an indispensable connection in the ecosystem of environmental wholeness; without the dump we would drown in our own refuse. Fundamentally the dump is a place of dissolution and renewal, the compost heap of the city. Because we ignore the dump's role in the circle of dwelling, the flow of materials through it is clogged. Like a good doctor, the dump is alerting us to the imbalances of the city's ecology, to the needs of conserving materials and recycling our waste. Whether or not we heed the garbage dump's call, the unseen powers that animate the physical world are working through it toward the dynamic balance of life's polarities; this is its sacredness.

An oil refinery can be seen in a similar light. It is a monster, polluting and threatening to ecological health; simultaneously it fuels the essentials of modern life—the movement of goods and services, plastic computer equipment, etc. The refinery warns us that our system of dwelling is destroying the very environment that sustains us. Likewise, a slum is the neglected, atrophying limb of the city. Similar to the overflowing garbage dump, it signals imbalances in the communal body; the vital juices of commerce, education, and political power are not flowing freely through the city. Ignoring one part of the organism jeopardizes the health of the entire system.

These messages may frighten or repulse us, but honoring them is essential to finding the sacred in everyday architecture. It is the equivalent of Hindus paying homage to the deity Shiva, whose dance is the universe. In Shiva's hair, a skull and new moon symbolize the coexistence of death and rebirth, the moment of becoming. One hand grips the drum of time, whose ticking veils the silence of eternity. But in the opposite hand, Shiva holds the flame of knowledge, which burns away the mask of time, opening our minds to the timeless. Similarly, the image of Christ being crucified on the cross goes beyond beauty and ugliness to present a symbol of the sublime that transcends aesthetic judgments. As described in Chapter One, the entrances to Japanese shrines are often flanked by two statues representing fear and desire, warding off those too fainthearted to make the spiritual quest. Passing between these twin pillars, we enter the sacred realm.

The sterile corridors of a hospital, the visual assault of a strip mall, the monotony of a freeway, and other offensive environments challenge our experience of sacredness. By having the courage to look deeply into the face of the ugly as well as the beautiful, however, our gaze can meet the eyes of the divine glistening behind every mask of architectural form.

This realization precedes meaningful renovation. Recognizing the sacred in the vile allows us to heal our relationship to the world here and now. We do not have to wait for our home or city to change before we experience its underlying wholeness. In fact it is only by fathoming the silent core of our own consciousness that we gain the clarity and openness that enable us to listen to the needs of the garbage dump, oil refinery, or slum. We cannot give what we do not have. Only by establishing ourselves in wholeness can we hope to build wholeness into the places that shelter us.

By perceiving the sacred in every facet of the surroundings, our minds become sacred. Each sight and sound reconnects the fragments of dwelling to the whole. Experiencing the energy and intelligence in wood and stone, we touch the soul of existence. Hearing silence in brick and mortar, we partake of life's silent core. Seeing light reflected in glass and steel, we become the light. Tasting the

Life in which objects predominate, where matter alone is found and values of the spirit or soul are overshadowed, is called material life. After enlightenment, the flower is seen, but the experience of the flower does not overshadow Being.
Maharishi Mahesh Yogi

sacred in all things, we ingest sacredness, metabolize it, and allow its wholeness to permeate our being.

Architecture comes to be known as an expression of our own consciousness. Distinctions between inner and outer fade. Aspiration is the brick and mortar of the steeple. Love is the stone of the sanctuary. Ultimately we realize that the sacred in architecture is not "out there" but "in here." Buildings do not surround us; our consciousness surrounds them. Like the spider who spins its web from within, the inner architect works the stuff of our own consciousness into myriad building forms, reenacting the primal creation.

> In the beginning there was only the Great Self in the form of a Person. Reflecting, it found nothing but itself. Then its first word was: "This am I!" . . . Then he realized: "I, indeed, am this creation; for I have poured it forth from myself." In that way he became this creation. And verily, he who knows this becomes in this creation a creator.　**Upanishads**

The self makes architecture from the self. The mind conceives a house to shelter itself. Consciousness is poured into every grain of the structure. Because the mind, like the world, is made of energy and information, I can know the architecture of the universe by exploring my own inner house. Bursting the roof of limited mental constructs, I see architecture as the mansion of my own consciousness. Instead of settling into a fixed condition with limited horizons, each structure becomes a flexible system of dwelling. Every form is opened to the formless sacred.

Entering the door to this realization, we return to our true home. The separations of heart and mind, consciousness and matter, self and other are transcended. The long search through the parched land of isolated objects has led to the sacred wellspring of the soul. Surprisingly enough, the journey leads to where it began, the temple of the spirit within our own house. As Heinrich Zimmer observed:

> The real treasure, that which can put an end to our poverty and all our trials, is never very far; there is no need to seek it in a distant country. It lies buried in the most intimate parts of our own house; that is of our own being. It is behind the stove, the center of life and warmth that rules our existence,

Know ye not that ye are the temple of God, and that the Spirit of God dwelleth in you.
The Apostle Paul

The scientist's religious feeling takes the form of a rapturous amazement at the harmony of natural law, which reveals an intelligence of such superiority that, in comparison with it, the highest intelligence of human beings is an utterly insignificant reflection.
Albert Einstein

the heart, if only we knew how to unearth it. And yet—there is this strange and persistent fact, that it is only after a pious journey in a distant region, in a new land, that the meaning of the inner voice guiding us on our search can make itself understood by us.

Finding the temple in the house is ultimately an awakening to the miracle of everyday circumstances, dead buildings resurrected by the power of our own consciousness. When we embrace the wholeness of inner spirit and outer form, the world, in its slightest detail, becomes an embodiment of eternity. The varied terrain of life is perceived as a harmonious, sacred place.

The pages of this book have pointed to new ways of seeing the juncture of consciousness and matter—discovering that mind, body, and architecture are different currents within the ocean of the soul. Its true value will be realized when these ways of seeing and creating are carried into the day-to-day comings and goings of the world. Then the wasteland can be healed, transformed into a land of wholeness. Spontaneously we see to the heart of things—finding the temple dwelling within every house, the shrine living in every garden, and the radiant spirit dancing in every particle of creation.

Anything that gives sensory experience to a room retrieves the soul from abstraction. A flower, a wooden table, a ceramic vase, a little earth, the necessary watering of a plant—with such gestures we have located this room on earth.
Robert Sardello

The essential function of art is to become personally enlightened, wise, and whole. Then as a consequence of the former function, the purpose of this wisdom, the purpose of art, is to make the community enlightened, wise, and whole.
Peter London

Acknowledgments

I express my gratitude to the people whose knowledge, assistance, and encouragement made this book possible: Maharishi Mahesh Yogi, whose wisdom about the integration of life provided the foundation; Suzanne Thomas Lawlor, for her sage advice and ability to keep the ideas grounded; my family, for their constant support; the people at Tarcher/Putnam, especially Jeremy Tarcher, for his expansive and compassionate vision, Daniel Malvin and Allen Mikaelian, for making the dream practical, Gregory Dobie, whose keen editing honed and strengthened the text, and Susan Shankin, for her insightful book design; my literary agent, Muriel Nellis, who combines brilliant business acumen with heart and wisdom, and her assistants, Jane Roberts and Karen Gerwin; my enlightened design partner, Sue Weller, for keeping the firm going while I wrote; and Martin Pasco, for the magnificent renderings.

I also thank the many people who have shared their thoughts and encouragement: Elaine Arnold, Ron Blair, Melanie Brown, Cindy Buck, Michael Cain, Ellen and Stan Deck, Toni d'Orr, Hada and Hadani, David T. Hanson, Robert Hoerlein, Sue and Peter Huggins, Jonathan Lipman and Pam Whitworth, Duncan MacMaster, Ali Najafi, Claudia and Mark Petrick, Marci Shimoff, Joanne and Fred Smith, Mike Tompkins, Mary Thomas Weiss, Rick Weller, Fauna and Phil White, Bill Witherspoon, Mary Zeilbeck, and others too numerous to mention.

Much appreciation goes to our clients, whose desire to enliven consciousness in their surroundings inspires my work, especially: Rona and Jeffrey Abramson, Susan and Larry Chroman, Josie and Paul Fauerso, Tim Fitz-Randolph, Gillian and Steven Foster, Susan Gore, Fred Gratzon, Francie and Doug Greenfield, Ann Hauptman, Bruce Hauptman, Debbie and Doug Henning, Christine and Steve Juskewycz, Susan and Jay Marcus, Malak and Nathan Otto, Debra and Fred Poneman, Karen and Steve Rubin, Suzanne and Carl Stone, Margie and Chris Wege, Mokie and Stuart Zimmerman. Special thanks to Buzz Ford, who has built many of our projects.

I thank the following institutions, photographers and architecture firms for their assistance in obtaining photographs: American Museum of Natural History; Dirk Bakker; Robert Benson; Boston Public Library; Robert Cameron; Andres Duany and Elizabeth Plater-Zyberk, Architects; Colleen Hennessy at the Freer Gallery of Art; HOK Sports Facilities Group; Library of Congress; Mississauga Civic Centre; Murphy/Jahn Architects; Museum of the City of New York; Arthur Olivas at the Museum of New Mexico; Andrea Gibbs at the National Gallery of Art; New York Public Library; Pei Cobb Freed & Partners; Mark Paul Petrick; Philadelphia Museum of Art; Dan Savaard at the Royal British Columbia Museum; Smithsonian Institution; Susan Mitchell at Team Disney; Venturi, Scott Brown and Associates; Paul Warchol.

List of Illustrations

Chapter Three. Steeple and Sanctuary

Chapter Four. The Eight Elemental Forms

Chapter Five. Mind ▪ Body ▪ Architecture

Chapter Six. Sunlight and Renewal

Chapter Seven. Making a Sacred Place

Chapter Eight. The Sacred City

Chapter Nine. Sacred World

Bibliography

Appelbaum, David, "Money and the City." *Parabola*, 16: 1, February 1991.

Ardalan, Nader, and Bakhtiar Laleh, *The Sense of Unity*. Chicago and London: University of Chicago Press, 1973.

Brown, Melanie, *Attaining Personal Greatness*. New York: William Morrow and Company, 1987.

———, Veronica Butler, and Nancy Lonsdorf, *A Woman's Best Medicine*. New York: Jeremy P. Tarcher/G. P. Putnam's Sons, 1993.

Bly, Robert, *The Kabir Book*. Boston: Beacon Press, 1977.

———, *News of the Universe*. San Francisco: Sierra Club Books, 1980.

Campbell, Joseph, *The Hero with a Thousand Faces*. Princeton, NJ: Princeton University Press, 1973.

———, *Historical Atlas of World Mythology, Vol. I, Part 2*. New York: Harper & Row, 1989.

———, *Historical Atlas of World Mythology, Vol. II, Part 3*. New York: Harper & Row, 1989.

———, *The Mythic Image*. Princeton, NJ: Princeton University Press, 1974.

Ching, Francis D. K., *Architecture: Form, Space and Order*. New York: Van Nostrand Reinhold Company, 1979.

Chopra, Deepak, *Perfect Health*. New York: Harmony Books, 1990.

———, *Quantum Healing*. New York: Bantam Books, 1989.

Dagens, Bruno, *Mayamata*. New Delhi: Sitaram Bhartia Institute of Scientific Research, 1985.

Doczi, György, *The Power of Limits*. Boulder and London: Shambhala Publications, 1981.

Eliade, Mircea, *The Sacred and the Profane*. New York: Harcourt Brace Jovanovich, 1987.

———, *Symbolism, the Sacred, and the Arts*. New York: Continuum, 1992.

Fletcher, Sir Banister, *A History of Architecture*. New York: Charles Scribner's Sons, 1954.

Gablik, Suzi, *The Reenchantment of Art*. New York: Thames and Hudson, 1991.

Halpern, Lawrence, *Cities*. Cambridge, MA: MIT Press, 1972.

Hamilton, Edith, *Mythology*. New York: Mentor, 1969.

Herchong, Lisa, *Thermal Delight in Architecture*. Cambridge, MA: MIT Press, 1979.

Holborn, Mark, *The Ocean in the Sand*. Boulder and London: Shambhala Publications, 1978.

Ions, Veronica, *Indian Mythology*. New York: Peter Bedrick Books, 1983.

Itoh, Teiji, *The Gardens of Japan*. Tokyo, New York, and San Francisco: Kodansha International, 1984.

———, *Space and Illusion in the Japanese Garden*. New York and Tokyo: Weatherhill/Tankosha, 1980.

Kostof, Spiro, *The Architect*. New York: Oxford University Press, 1985.

———, *A History of Architecture*. New York: Oxford University Press, 1985.

Lame Deer, John (Fire), and Richard Erdoes, *Lame Deer, Seeker of Visions*. New York: Pocket Books, 1972.

Lawlor, Robert, *Sacred Geometry*. New York: Crossroad Publishing Company, 1982.

Lifchez, Raymond, *The Dervish Lodge*. Berkeley: University of California Press, 1992.

Lobell, John, *Between Silence and Light: Spirit in the Architecture of Louis I. Kahn*. Boulder and London: Shambhala Publications, 1979.

MacNulty, W. Kirk, *Freemasonry*. London: Thames and Hudson, 1991.

Maharishi Mahesh Yogi, *On the Bhagavad-Gita*. Baltimore: Penguin Books, 1969.

————, *The Science of Being and Art of Living*. London: International SRM Publications, 1967.

Michell, George, *The Hindu Temple*. Chicago and London: University of Chicago Press, 1988.

Mitchell, Stephen, *The Enlightened Heart*. New York: Harper & Row, 1989.

————, *The Enlightened Mind*. New York: Harper & Row, 1991.

————, *Tao te Ching*. New York: Harper & Row, 1988.

Mookerjee, Ajit, *Ritual Art of India*. New York: Thames and Hudson, 1985.

————, and Madhu Khanna, *The Tantric Way*. Boston: New York Graphic Society, 1977.

Moore, Charles, and Gerald Allen, *Dimensions*. New York: Architectural Record Books, 1976.

Moore, Thomas, *The Care of the Soul*. New York: HarperCollins Publishers, 1992.

Moyne, John, and Coleman Barks, *Open Secret: Versions of Rumi*. Putney, VT: Threshold Books, 1984.

Nabokov, Peter, and Robert Easton, *Native American Architecture*. New York: Oxford University Press, 1989.

Nhat Hanh, Thich, *The Heart of Understanding*. Berkeley: Parallax Press, 1988.

Palladio, Andrea, *The Four Books of Architecture*. New York: Dover Publications, 1965.

Pennick, Nigel, *Sacred Geometry*. Wellingborough, Northamptonshire: Turnstone Press Limited, 1980.

Puppi, Lionello, *Andrea Palladio*. Boston: New York Graphic Society, 1975.

Reps, Paul, *Zen Flesh, Zen Bones*. Garden City, NY: Anchor Books, 1961.

Robbins, Tom, *Skinny Legs and All*. New York: Bantam Books, 1991.

Rossbach, Sarah, *Feng Shui: The Chinese Art of Placement*. New York: E. P. Dutton, 1983.

Sardello, Robert, *Facing the World with Soul*. Hudson, NY: Lindisfarne Press, 1992.

Smithsonian Exposition Books, *Fire of Life*. New York and London: W. W. Norton and Company, 1981.

Snodgrass, Adrian, *The Symbolism of the Stupa*. Delhi: Motilal Banarsidass Publishers, 1992.

Snyder, Gary, *The Practice of the Wild*. San Francisco: North Point Press, 1990.

Swan, James A., *The Power of Place*. Wheaton, IL: Quest Books, 1991.

Tanaka, Seno, *The Tea Ceremony*. New York: Harmony Books, 1977.

Tanizaki, Junichiro, *In Praise of Shadows*. New Haven: Leete's Island Books, 1977.

Wittkower, Rudolf, *Architectural Principles in the Age of Humanism*. New York and London: W. W. Norton and Company, 1971.

Yanagi, Soetsu, *The Unknown Craftsman*. Tokyo, New York, and San Francisco: Kodansha International, 1972.

Index